WJEC EDUQAS

# English Literature

Margaret Graham

Endorsed by

eduqas
Part of WJEC

OXFORD
UNIVERSITY PRESS

# OXFORD
#### UNIVERSITY PRESS

Great Clarendon Street, Oxford, OX2 6DP, United Kingdom

Oxford University Press is a department of the University of Oxford. It furthers the University's objective of excellence in research, scholarship, and education by publishing worldwide. Oxford is a registered trade mark of Oxford University Press in the UK and in certain other countries

British Library Cataloguing in Publication Data

Data available

ISBN 978-019-833284-8

10 9 8 7 6 5 4 3 2 1

Printed in Great Britain by Ashford Print and Publishing Services, Gosport

## Acknowledgements

The author and publisher are grateful for permission to reprint the following copyright material:

**Maya Angelou:** 'On Ageing' from *And Still I Rise* (Virago, 1986) copyright © Maya Angelou 1978, reprinted by permission of the publishers, Little Brown Book Group Ltd and Random House an imprint and division of Penguin Random House LLC. All rights reserved.

**Simon Armitage:** extracts from 'The Manhunt' from *The Not Dead* (Pomona, 2008), copyright © Simon Armitage 2008, reprinted by permission of the publishers.

**Alan Bennett:** extract from *The History Boys* (Faber, 2004), reprinted by permission of Faber & Faber Ltd

**Shelagh Delaney:** extract from Act 2 Scene 1, *A Taste of Honey* (Methuen Drama, 1982) copyright © Shelagh Delaney 1959, reprinted by permission of the publishers, Bloomsbury Publishing Plc.

**Carol Ann Duffy:** extracts from 'Valentine' from *Mean Time* (Picador, 2013), copyright © Carol Ann Duffy 1993, 2013, reprinted by permission of the author c/o Rogers, Coleridge & White Ltd, 20 Powis Mews, London W11 1JN

**James Fenton:** 'Nothing' from *Yellow Tulips* (Faber, 2013), reprinted by permission of Faber & Faber Ltd

**Zulfikar Ghose:** 'Decomposition' from *Selected Poems* (OUP, 1991), copyright © Zulfikar Ghose 1967, reprinted by permission of Sheil Land Associates Ltd on behalf of the author.

**William Golding:** extract from *Lord of the Flies* (Faber, 2009), copyright © William Golding 1954, reprinted by permission of Faber & Faber Ltd

**Greg Hill:** 'Shopkeeper' from *Poetry Wales*, volume 31, no 3, reprinted by permission of the author.

**Susan Hill:** extract from *The Woman in Black* (Vintage, 1998), copyright © Susan Hill 1983, reprinted by permission of Sheil Land Associates Ltd.

**Rupert M Loydell:** 'Tramp' from *Fill These Days* (Stride, 1990), copyright © Rupert M Loydell 1990, reprinted by permission of the author.

**Gareth Owen:** 'Song of the City' from *Song of the City* (Collins, 1985), reprinted by permission of Pollinger Ltd (www.pollingerltd.com) on behalf of the author.

**Brian Patten:** 'The River's Story' from *Thawing Frozen Frogs* (Puffin, 2e 2003), copyright © Brian Patten 1990, reprinted by permission of the author c/o Rogers, Coleridge & White Ltd, 20 Powis Mews, London W11 1JN.

**Simon Stephens and Mark Haddon:** extract from Act 1, *The Curious Incident of the Dog in the Night-Time* (Methuen Drama, 2013), copyright © Simon Stephens and Mark Haddon 2013, reprinted by permission of the publishers, Bloomsbury Publishing Plc.

**David Sutton:** 'Another Small Incident' from *Flints* (Peterloo, 1986), copyright © David Sutton 1986, reprinted by permission of the author

**Matthew Sweeney:** 'Zero Hour' from *Sanctuary* (Cape, 2004), copyright © Matthew Sweeney 2004, reprinted by permission of The Random House Group Ltd.

**H G Wells:** extract from *The War of the Worlds* (Heinemann,1898), reprinted by permission of United Agents LLP on behalf of The Literary Executors of the Estate of H G Wells, and of Ollie Record Productions.

**Jeanette Winterson:** extract from *Oranges Are Not the Only Fruit* (Vintage, 2010), copyright © Jeanette Winterson 1985, reprinted by permission of The Random House Group Ltd.

The author and publisher would like to thank the following for permission to use their photographs:

**Cover image:** © Extreme Sports Photo/Alamy; **p10-11:** Oli Scarff/Getty Images; **p12:** © Geraint Lewis/Alamy; **p15:** Alastair Muir/REX; **p16:** © Geraint Lewis/Alamy; **p18-19:** Blend Images/REX; **p21:** Hiroyuki Ito/Getty Images; **p23:** Sarah L. Voisin/The Washington Post via Getty Images; **p25:** © AF archive/Alamy; **p26-27:** Hulton Archive/Stringer/Getty; **p30-31:** Aldo Murillo/iStockphoto; **p33:** Scott Barbour/Getty Images; **p35:** Emily Goodwin/Shutterstock; **p36-37:** Nazar Yosyfiv/Shutterstock; **p39:** Dimas Ardian/Bloomberg via Getty Images; **p40-41:** © Ernie Janes/Alamy; **p43t:** © AF archive/Alamy; **p43b:** © Richard Matthews/Alamy; **p45:** © L A Heusinkveld/Alamy; **p46:** Kemie/iStock; **p47:** BeholdingEye/iStock; **p49:** © Rolf Nussbaumer/Nature Picture Library/Corbis; **p51:** Carl D. Walsh/Portland Press Herald via Getty Images; **p53:** © Penny Tweedie/Alamy; **p55:** © AfriPics.com/Alamy; **p57:** Major Evarts Tracey/Keystone/Getty Images; **p59:** eugen_Z/iStock; **p60-61:** Nika Art/Shutterstock; **p62-63:** Soldt/iStock; **p64:** DeAgostini/Getty Images; **p65:** Vlad Siaber/Shutterstock; **p66:** Ivonne Wierink/Shutterstock; **p67:** NEIL ROY JOHNSON/Shutterstock; **p68-69:** Olha Rohulya/Shutterstock; **p70-71:** © Photostage; **p75:** © Photostage; **p77:** arosoft/Shutterstock; **p78:** © Photostage; **p79:** © AF archive/Alamy; **p80:** © Photostage; **p81:** © AF archive/Alamy; p82: Alastair Muir/REX; p83: © Photostage; p84: Daniel Gale/Shutterstock; **p85:** © Photostage; **p86-87:** Nejron Photo/Shutterstock; **p89:** © Lebrecht Music and Arts Photo Library/Alamy; **p93:** © Moviestore collection Ltd/Alamy; **p94-95:** © AF archive/Alamy; **p96:** Museum of London; **p97:** Public Domain; **p99:** BBC Photo Library; **p100:** BBC Photo Library; **p102:** © AF archive/Alamy; **p105:** Moviestore collection Ltd/Alamy; **p106:** © Photos 12/Alamy; **p107:** © DAVID NEWHAM/Alamy; **p110:** © Corbis; **p114:** © World History Archive/Alamy; **p116-117:** Snap Stills/REX; **p118-119:** Ed Samuel/Shutterstock; **p120:** oknoart/Shutterstock; **p123:** Snap Stills/REX; **p125:** © LOOK Die Bildagentur der Fotografen GmbH/Alamy; **p127:** © Dave Bevan/Alamy; **p128-129:** © Prisma Bildagentur AG/Alamy; **p130:** © Barry Diomede/Alamy; **p131:** Tischenko Irina/Shutterstock; **p133:** © MBI/Alamy; **p135t:** © Pawel Bienkowski/Alamy; **p135b:** © ClassicStock/Alamy; **p138:** © Gianni Muratore/Alamy; **p140-141:** pixcolo/iStock; **p142-143:** Vipavlenkoff/Shutterstock.

Although we have made every effort to trace and contact all copyright holders before publication this has not been possible in all cases. If notified, the publisher will rectify any errors or omissions at the earliest opportunity.

Designed and produced by Ian Foulis Design.

# CONTENTS

# INTRODUCTION

## WJEC Eduqas GCSE English Literature specification overview

### What you will be studying

Across the two GCSE English Literature Components, you will be studying the following:

- a Shakespeare play
- The WJEC Eduqas Poetry Anthology
- Post-1914 prose or drama
- A 19th-century novel
- Unseen poetry.

### What you will be learning

During your course you will be learning:

- how to analyse the way the writers have created meanings
- how to show an understanding of the relationships between some of the texts and their contexts
- how to compare poems.

### The exam papers

The grade you receive at the end of your WJEC Eduqas GCSE English Literature course is entirely based on your performance in two exam papers. The following provides a summary of these two exam papers:

| Exam paper | Questions and marks | Assessment Objectives | Timing | Marks (and % of GCSE) |
|---|---|---|---|---|
| **Component 1: Shakespeare** | **Section A: Shakespeare** <br> **Exam texts:** <br> *Romeo and Juliet*; OR *Macbeth*; OR *Othello*; OR *Much Ado About Nothing*; OR *Henry V*; OR *The Merchant of Venice* <br> Exam questions and marks: <br> One extract question [15 marks] and one essay based on the reading of a Shakespeare text from the above list [25 marks] | • AO1 <br> • AO2 <br> • AO4 [in essay only] | 2 hours | Section A: 40 marks (20% GCSE) |
| **Poetry** | **Section B: Poetry from 1789 to the present day** <br> Two questions based on poems from the WJEC Eduqas Poetry Anthology, one of which involves comparison <br> Exam questions and marks: <br> Response to first poem (printed on paper) [15 marks] <br> Response to second poem (own choice) and comparison with first poem [25 marks] | • AO1 <br> • AO2 <br> • AO3 | | Section B: 40 marks (20% GCSE) <br><br> Component 1 total: 80 marks (40% GCSE) |

| Exam paper | Questions and marks | Assessment Objectives | Timing | Marks (and % of GCSE) |
|---|---|---|---|---|
| **Component 2: Post-1914 prose/drama** | **Section A: Post-1914 prose/drama**<br>**Exam texts:** *Lord of the Flies* (Golding); OR *Anita and Me* (Syal); OR *Never Let Me Go* (Ishiguro); OR *The Woman in Black* (Hill); OR *Oranges Are Not the Only Fruit* (Winterson); OR *The Curious Incident of the Dog in the Night-Time* (play script) (Stephens); OR *A Taste of Honey* (Delaney); OR *An Inspector Calls* (Priestley); OR *The History Boys* (Bennett); OR *Blood Brothers* (Russell)<br>Exam questions and marks:<br>One source-based question on one of the above texts [40 marks] | • AO1<br>• AO2<br>• AO4 | 2 hours 30 mins | Section A: 40 marks (20% GCSE) |
| **19th-century prose** | **Section B: 19th-century prose**<br>**Exam texts:** *A Christmas Carol* (Dickens); OR *Silas Marner* (Eliot); OR *War of the Worlds* (H.G. Wells); OR *Pride and Prejudice* (Austen); OR *Jane Eyre* (Brontë); OR *The Strange Case of Dr Jekyll and Mr Hyde* (Stevenson)<br>Exam question and marks:<br>One source-based question on one of the above texts [40 marks] | • AO1<br>• AO2<br>• AO3 | | Section B: 40 marks (20% GCSE) |
| **Unseen poetry** | **Section C: Unseen poetry from the 20th/21st centuries**<br>Exam question and marks:<br>Response to first printed poem [15 marks]<br>Response to second printed poem and comparison with first poem [25 marks] | • AO1<br>• AO2 | | Section C: 40 marks (20% GCSE)<br>Component 2 total: 120 marks (60% GCSE) |

## The Poetry Anthology

As part of your GCSE English Literature course you will be studying an anthology of poetry. To support the Poetry Anthology, WJEC Eduqas has produced a CD-ROM of poetry support material that includes the poems, different audio recordings of the poems and images to stimulate discussion of the poems. The CD-ROM and the Poetry Anthology are available for teachers to order, free of charge, from WJEC Eduqas.

# Introduction to this book

## How this book will help you

### Develop your knowledge, understanding and appreciation of a range of novels, drama and poetry

The primary aim of this book is to develop and improve your understanding of English Literature, in the context of what the exam papers will be asking of you at the end of your course. So, the skills you will be practising throughout this book are ideal preparation for your two English Literature exam papers.

### Explore the texts that you will face in the exams

In your English Literature exams you will have to respond to a number of texts. In order to prepare you fully for the texts that you will face in the exam, this book is structured so you can develop your understanding of the different types of text, novels, plays and poetry, through a range of activities.

### Become familiar with the Assessment Objectives and the exam paper requirements

Assessment Objectives are the skills that underpin all qualifications. Your knowledge and skills will be tested in the exams using four Assessment Objectives (AOs). Sections 1 to 5 of this book develop the necessary skills, in the context of these Assessment Objectives.

| AO1 | Read, understand and respond to texts. Students should be able to:<br>• maintain a critical style and develop an informed personal response<br>• use textual references, including quotations, to support and illustrate interpretations |
|---|---|
| AO2 | Analyse the language, form and structure used by a writer to create meanings and effects, using relevant terminology where appropriate |
| AO3 | Show understanding of the relationships between texts and the contexts in which they are written |
| AO4 | Use a range of vocabulary and sentence structures for clarity, purpose and effect, with accurate spelling and punctuation |

### Practise the types of task you will face in the exams

Sections 1 to 5 of this book include activities that enable you to demonstrate what you have learned and help your teacher assess your progress.

## How is the book structured?

### Sections 1 to 5

Sections 1 to 5 develop your understanding of the texts you will meet in the different sections of the exam. Each section opens with two introductory pages that explain the skills you will be developing and link the learning to the exam requirements.

The sections then include a range of activities to help you develop your skills in English Literature.

## What are the main features in this book?

### Activities, Support and Stretch

To develop your reading responses to the wide range of texts included in this book as well as developing your writing skills, you will find many varied activities. The 'Support' feature provides additional help with some activities while the 'Stretch' feature introduces a further challenge to help develop a more advanced response.

### Tips, Key terms and glossed words

These features help support your understanding of key terms, concepts and more difficult words within a source text. These therefore enable you to concentrate fully on developing your reading and writing skills.

### Exam link and Progress check

The 'Exam link' box explains how the skills you are developing relate to the exam papers. In addition to summative sample exam question tasks, you will also find regular formative assessments in the form of 'Progress checks'. These enable you to establish, through peer or self-assessment, how confident you feel about what you have been learning.

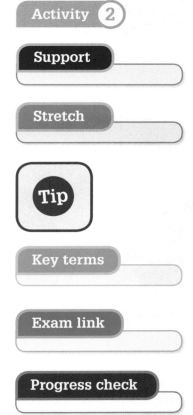

Activity 2

Support

Stretch

Tip

Key terms

Exam link

Progress check

> **A note on spelling**
> Certain words, for example 'summarize' and 'organize', have been spelt with 'ize' throughout this book. It is equally acceptable to spell these words with 'ise'.

# Further GCSE English Language and GCSE English Literature resources

### WJEC Eduqas GCSE English Language Student Book 1: Developing the skills for Component 1 and Component 2

Student Book 1 develops vital reading and writing skills in engaging thematic contexts while also focusing on the Assessment Objectives linked to the requirements of the exams. This book is ideal for the start of the GCSE course and features:

- development of in-depth reading and writing skills in thematic contexts
- differentiated support and stretch activities with an embedded focus on technical accuracy
- Assessment Objective focus linked to the requirements of the exams
- opportunities for peer and self-assessment
- regular formative and summative assessments, including sample exam papers.

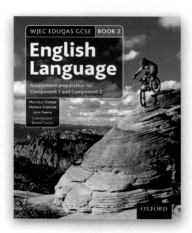

### WJEC Eduqas GCSE English Language Student Book 2: Assessment preparation for Component 1 and Component 2

Student Book 2 provides you with all the exam preparation and practice that you need to succeed. The book is divided into Reading and Writing sections and further divided into chapters which guide you through the Assessment Objective and exam paper question requirements. The book features:

- a range of texts and tasks similar to those you will encounter in the exam
- activities to practise and reinforce the key skills with advice on how to improve your responses
- marked sample student responses at different levels
- opportunities for peer and self-assessment
- sample exam papers.

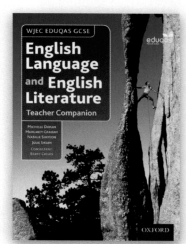

### WJEC Eduqas GCSE English Language and English Literature Teacher Companion

The Teacher Companion provides holistic support for teachers to help them plan and deliver their GCSE programme, including:

- specification insight and planning guidance to aid planning and delivery of the specifications
- teaching tips and guidance for effective lesson delivery to all students of the material in Student Book 1, with additional support for differentiation and personalization
- extensive exam preparation guidance and planning with links to English Language Student Book 2 and English Literature Student Book
- guidance and support for delivering Spoken Language assessments
- links to, and guidance on, the additional resources on Kerboodle.

# WJEC Eduqas GCSE English Language and English Literature Kerboodle: Resources and Assessment

## What is Kerboodle?

Kerboodle is a brand new online subscription-based platform provided by Oxford University Press.

## Kerboodle: Resources and Assessment

WJEC Eduqas GCSE English Language and English Literature Kerboodle: Resources and Assessment provides comprehensive support and resources to enable English departments and individual teachers to plan their GCSE courses and deliver effective, personalized lessons that prepare students for the requirements of the exams. Resources include:

- Teaching and learning materials, linked to the corresponding Student Books and Teacher Companion, including:
  - differentiation, personalization and peer/self-assessment worksheets and teaching resources
  - a bank of spelling, punctuation and grammar interactive activities to improve technical accuracy.

- Assessment resources, including:
  - marked sample answers to the Student Book 1 and Student Book 2 assessments, with mark schemes
  - editable versions of the end-of-section Student Book assessments and sample exam papers.

- Professional development materials, including:
  - six specially-commissioned film-based CPD units written by Geoff Barton with classroom lesson footage, additional interviews (with Phil Jarrett and Michelle Doran) and supporting written resources – ideal for departmental meetings
  - a comprehensive grammar guide for GCSE teaching.

- Planning resources, including:
  - editable sample schemes of work and medium-term plans, with guidance on what to consider when planning your GCSE course
  - CPD units supporting discussion around departmental GCSE planning.

- Digital books including:
  - all three Student Books in digital format*
  - a bank of tools enabling personalization.

*Also available individually for student access

# 1 Shakespeare

## Assessment Objectives

- **AO1** Read, understand and respond to the text, maintaining a critical style, developing a personal response, and using textual references, including quotations, to support and illustrate interpretations

- **AO2** Analyse the language, form and structure used by a writer to create meanings and effects, using relevant subject terminology where appropriate

- **AO4** Use a range of vocabulary and sentence structures for clarity, purpose and effect, with accurate spelling and punctuation (essay only)

In this section of the book, you will develop the skills needed to write about the Shakespeare play you are studying. You will get plenty of practice in developing the skills necessary to tackle the exam questions, by:

- summing up the main ideas
- exploring characters' speech and behaviour
- discussing key themes and the creation of mood and atmosphere, while all the time thinking about how the play is written and structured.

# In the exam

You will need to show your close-reading skills by discussing in detail an extract from the play, which will be printed on the exam paper. You will then show your understanding of the play as a whole, by writing an extended essay.

You will look closely at the printed extract from the play you have studied (*Henry V*, *Macbeth*, *Much Ado About Nothing*, *Othello*, *Romeo and Juliet* or *The Merchant of Venice*) and answer a question focused on the extract. This may be on:

- its dramatic impact
- the creation of mood and atmosphere
- the speech and behaviour of one or more of the characters.

You will then go on to discuss the effects this may have on an audience.

You will also write a detailed response to a question about the play as a whole. You will need to show:

- a sound knowledge of the story of the play, particularly its main events
- an understanding of the characters and their relationships
- an understanding of the themes of the play, and the way these are put across by Shakespeare.

You should spend about an hour on these questions in the exam. It is a good idea to spend about 20 minutes on the extract and about 40 minutes on the essay. Jot down a reminder about these timings before you start writing in the exam!

## Extract

- Remember that although the focus is on the printed extract, it's fine to show that you know how it fits into the play as a whole – what happened before and what will happen after – as long as you deal with this in no more than a sentence or two.

- Focus closely on the question from the start: if the question asks you about the mood and atmosphere, be specific (and remember that the mood and atmosphere may change, even in a short extract). If the question asks about the presentation of a character, make a range of specific points. If it asks about thoughts and feelings (either of a character or of an audience) break your answer down into particular thoughts and feelings, too.

- Select words and phrases (the shorter the better) from throughout the extract to back up your points.

- Don't be tempted to launch into a full essay – keep focused on the extract throughout.

- You should spend about 20 minutes on this (including reading, thinking, and making notes).

## Essay

- Aim to have a clear, strong start, focusing on the question from the beginning.

- Keep referring to the question all the way through (at least in every paragraph).

- It's fine to take a chronological approach, starting with events at the start of the play, and working through to the end, as long as you keep focused on the question and don't just tell the story.

- If you can, keep a good point back, so that you can end the essay strongly.

- You should spend about 40 minutes on the essay.

# 1 Sorting out the story

## Learning objective

- To understand the key areas of a Shakespeare play, by forming an overview of each act, and backing this up with selected details

All Shakespeare plays are made up of five acts. As you read the play, you should make notes for each act, using the following headings:

- What happens – make this as **succinct** as possible, summing up the content of the act in as few sentences as possible.

- Where it is set – with brief comments if relevant. Remember that there may be different settings for scenes within the act.

- The purpose of each scene within the act – for example, a scene may move the plot on, introduce a character, or change the mood and atmosphere.

- The main characters involved, with a few comments on first impressions of them.

- The high points of each act – maybe in the form of brief quotations and comments. Aim for no more than ten.

Opposite is an example of what notes for the first act of *Macbeth* might look like.

### Activity 1

a. Working on your own or with someone else, make notes similar to these on the opening act of the play you are studying.

b. Then, as you read the play, make the same kind of notes on the other four acts.

c. By the time you have finished these, you will have produced your own summary of the play.

| Overview of *Macbeth* Act 1 | |
|---|---|
| **What happens** | The audience hears of Macbeth and Banquo's warlike behaviour in battle, and King Duncan rewards Macbeth by making him Thane of Cawdor. Then three witches make prophecies to Macbeth and Banquo, including hailing Macbeth as Thane of Cawdor. Banquo is sceptical but Macbeth is intrigued, and when he sends a letter to his wife she sees no reason why he cannot fulfil the final prophecy, that he will be King, although she knows she will need to push him. By the end of the act, she has managed to persuade him to kill Duncan while he stays with them. |
| **Settings** | • wasteland – where the witches appear<br>• battlefield, after the defeat of the Norwegian army<br>• the king's palace – where Macbeth is promoted<br>• Macbeth's castle in Glamis |
| **Purpose of scenes** | 1: Introduces witches and links them with Macbeth.<br>2: Thane of Cawdor's treachery reported; Macbeth praised by King Duncan.<br>3: Witches make prophecies to Macbeth and Banquo. The seed of ambition is planted. Contrast between Macbeth and Banquo.<br>4: Duncan makes Malcolm Prince of Cumberland. Macbeth knows that he cannot leave his fate to chance.<br>5: Introduces Lady Macbeth and shows how well she understands her husband.<br>6: Duncan enters Macbeth's castle – never to leave.<br>7: Macbeth has doubts but Lady Macbeth quashes them; she has made her plans. |
| **Main characters** | • witches – introduce supernatural theme and its link to Macbeth<br>• Macbeth – reported as being ruthless soldier, but Lady Macbeth has doubts about his will to achieve ambitions<br>• Banquo – sensible and balanced<br>• Duncan – rather naïve?<br>• Lady Macbeth – determined and persuasive |
| **Points linked to key quotations** | • 'Fair is foul and foul is fair' – the witches. This is an upside-down world, and appearances can't be trusted.<br>• 'brave Macbeth (well he deserves that name)' – the bleeding Captain to Duncan and his son Malcolm. Irony?<br>• 'So foul and fair a day I have not seen.' – Macbeth echoing the witches' words. Showing a connection?<br>• 'And oftentimes, to win us to our harm,/The instruments of darkness tell us truths/Win us with honest trifles, to betray's/In deepest consequences' – Banquo already suspicious.<br>• 'Stars, hide your fires!/Let not light see my black and deep desires!' – Macbeth struggling with temptation.<br>• 'Glamis thou art, and Cawdor – and shalt be/What thou art promised! – Yet do I fear thy nature.' Lady Macbeth recognizes the job she has to do.<br>• '...never/Shall sun that morrow see!' – Lady Macbeth is determined that Duncan will not leave.<br>• 'I have no spur/To prick the sides of my intent, but only/vaulting ambition' –Macbeth having doubts?<br>• 'When you durst do it, then you were a man!' – Lady Macbeth works on her husband.<br>• 'I am settled – and bend up/Each corporal agent to this terrible feat' – Macbeth is persuaded. |

### Activity 2

#### Condensed Shakespeare

Now you have sorted out the key points of the play in some detail, you are going to summarize the play as succinctly as possible. Below is an example of a summary of *Romeo and Juliet* in 100 words.

> *The love between, and deaths of, two teenagers reunites two long-warring families – or does it?*
>
> Romeo Montague, disguised, attends the party of his family's enemy, the Capulets, where he falls in love with Juliet Capulet, and she with him. Juliet's cousin, Tybalt, challenges Romeo, but Romeo and Juliet are already secretly married, helped by her Nurse and Friar Lawrence. Angry Mercutio takes the challenge for Romeo, and is killed. Romeo kills Tybalt and is banished. Juliet takes a potion to avoid marrying Paris, but the plan fails, and she seems dead. Romeo goes to die with her, kills Paris, and himself. Juliet awakes too late and stabs herself to die with Romeo. Only Benvolio lives.

Now sum up the story of the Shakespeare play you have studied in 100 words or fewer. You may also use up to 15 words to provide a title for your summary. Think about the choices you had to make. Are any important parts of the play missing? Why did you choose some parts or characters rather than others?

#### Stretch

Now, the ultimate challenge: try to sum up the essence of the Shakespeare play you have studied in a tweet – 140 characters maximum, including spaces. Again, consider how many essential elements you managed to include, and what you had to leave out.

Here is how a *Romeo and Juliet* tweet might appear:

---

 **Kirsty**@kwalton · **Following**

Romeo Montague and Juliet Capulet, of enemy families, meet, fall in love, and die, partly through fate and partly through rashness.

**FAVOURITES** 21

8.16 AM – 10 Aug

---

## Activity 3

Working on your own, or with someone else, write programme notes for a production of the Shakespeare play you are studying, summing up each Act in just a few sentences. Remember to give an outline of each Act, so that an audience member would have an idea what is going on, without giving it all away.

For example, the programme notes for Act 1 of Macbeth may read like this:

> Close friends Macbeth and Banquo, wearied after a bloody battle which they won for their king, Duncan, meet strange creatures who make even stranger predictions to them. When Duncan arrives to stay with the Macbeths, Lady Macbeth decides to give fate a push, to make her husband's prediction come true.

### Exam link

Good answers include both *overview* (summing up points as briefly as possible) and *detail* to support and prove what you have said.

### Support

Find an illustration to match each Act, or draw your own.

# 2 Close focus on detail

## Learning objective

- To practise selecting and highlighting details of the Shakespeare play

Whether you are analysing a specified extract in an exam, or reading parts of the play in close detail in order to support your discussion of characters or themes, getting close to Shakespeare's language is the key to showing your deep understanding of the play you have studied.

Here, you will learn to develop these close reading skills, by annotating important extracts from the play.

### Key terms

**Soliloquy:** a speech where a character confides their thoughts to the audience, unheard by other characters

**Alliteration:** repetition of initial consonants for a specific effect

**Sibilance:** a sort of hissing sound, created by repeating 's' or 'sh' sounds

**Tip** The speech by Macbeth quoted on page 17 is a **soliloquy**, where a character speaks their innermost thoughts. It can give the audience an insight into their secret thoughts and feelings. See if you can find one or more examples of characters speaking in a soliloquy in the play you have studied (there are others in *Macbeth*, too) and see what they show you about the innermost thoughts of the character who speaks them. You may decide to use this speech for Activity 1.

### Activity 1

a. Choose a part of the play that you have studied that you think shows something interesting about a character or characters, or creates a strong mood and atmosphere for an audience, and try to annotate it in the way the extract from *Macbeth* is annotated on page 17.

b. Remember to use the whole extract; beginning, middle and end – so you will have to select the most important parts, and the words and phrases that really stand out.

### Exam link

The sort of annotations made on page 17 could be useful for a range of purposes, such as closely analysing an extract in order to show how Shakespeare creates mood and atmosphere for an audience, or to explore how a character is presented to an audience, or to support an answer on the whole play, focusing on character or theme.

Look at how this extract from *Macbeth* has been annotated, highlighting language and its effects.

**Macbeth** [*Aside*] ···◄············································ Sense of secrecy

                   Two truths are told,

Covering himself ·····► As happy prologues to the swelling act ◄····· Imagery associated with putting on a performance

Of the imperial theme.— I thank you, gentlemen.—

**Alliteration**: 's' sounds create ···► This supernatural soliciting

**sibilance** – sounds like sinister whispering ···· Cannot be ill, cannot be good. If ill,

Why hath it given me earnest of success,

Commencing in a truth? I am Thane of Cawdor. ◄····· The only certainty at the moment; strong rhythm in second half of line sounds emphatic

A long sentence – suggestive of excitement, or panic? ···► If good, why do I yield to that suggestion

Whose horrid image doth unfix my hair

And make my seated heart knock at my ribs

I.e. unnatural ····► Against the use of nature? Present fears

Are less than horrible imaginings: ◄····· Power of imagination

First mention of murder ···· My thought, whose murder yet is but fantastical,

Shakes so my single state of man that function

Is smother'd in surmise, and nothing is, ◄····· More sibilance

Almost feels paralyzed? ····► But what is not.

**Banquo**

               ► Look, how our partner's rapt.

Broken lines shared between Macbeth and Banquo – show how close they are. Can you find one more? **Macbeth**

If chance will have me king, why, chance may crown me

Without my stir. ◄····· Seems to be leaving it to fate

**Banquo**

         ► New honours come upon him

Banquo makes excuses for him. Note clothing imagery – appearance vs reality? ···► Like our strange garments, cleave not to their mould,

But with the aid of use.

**Macbeth**

            Come what come may, ◄····· Whatever will be, will be?

Time and the hour runs through the roughest day.

## Key term

**Stage directions:** instructions written into the script of the play, to help actors and people involved in producing the play understand how they should perform the scene in order to convey the characters, mood and atmosphere to an audience. They are often written in italics, or sometimes in brackets, to make them stand out from the dialogue

**Tip** There are plenty of different ways of interpreting Shakespeare's plays and the characters in them, so don't worry if your interpretation is different from other people's, as long as you can give reasons for what you say.

Shakespeare, unlike modern dramatists, rarely wrote **stage directions**. Indeed, when you read stage directions in an edition of one of his plays, they were probably inserted long after the play was written. In the example below, stage directions have been added to an extract from Act 1 Scene 5 of *Romeo and Juliet*.

## Activity 2

a. Choose an extract from the play you are studying and add your own stage directions (or the ones you think Shakespeare might have included if he had used them!).

b. This will help you to understand better how this part of the play might appear on stage and how the character may be feeling.

| | |
|---|---|
| **Romeo** | (Speaking to himself, watching Juliet dancing) |
| | O she doth teach the torches to burn bright! |
| | It seems she hangs upon the cheek of night |
| | Like a rich jewel in an Ethiope's ear— |
| | Beauty too rich for use, for earth too dear! |
| | So shows a snowy dove trooping with crows, |
| | As yonder lady o'er her fellows shows. |
| | The measure done, I'll watch her place of stand, |
| | And touching hers, make blessed my rude hand. |
| | Did my heart love till now? forswear it, sight! |
| | For I ne'er saw true beauty till this night. |
| **Tybalt** | (Overhearing Romeo) |
| | This, by his voice, should be a Montague. |
| | (Speaking to servant) |
| | Fetch me my rapier, boy. (To himself) What dares the slave |
| | Come hither, cover'd with an antic face, |
| | To fleer and scorn at our solemnity? |
| | Now, (Passionately) by the stock and honour of my kin, |
| | To strike him dead I hold it not a sin. |
| **Capulet** | (In a jovial mood) |
| | Why, how now, kinsman! wherefore storm you so? |
| **Tybalt** | Uncle, this is a Montague, our foe: |
| | A villain that is hither come in spite, |
| | To scorn at our solemnity this night. |
| | (Pointing at Romeo. Very excited, as if telling tales) |

**Capulet**   (In an interested tone)

Young Romeo is it?

**Tybalt**   'Tis he, that villain Romeo.

**Capulet**   (Placing a hand on Tybalt's shoulder, as if to calm him down)

Content thee, gentle coz, let him alone,

'A bears him like a portly gentleman;

And to say truth, Verona brags of him

To be a virtuous and well-govern'd youth.

(Speaking with determination)

I would not for the wealth of all the town

Here in my house do him disparagement;

Therefore be patient, take no note of him;

(Increasing in tone, becoming more assertive)

It is my will, the which if thou respect,

Show a fair presence and put off these frowns,

And ill-beseeming semblance for a feast.

**Tybalt**   (Shrugging away from Capulet)

It fits, when such a villain is a guest:

I'll not endure him.

**Capulet**   (Speaking determinedly. During this speech, he becomes increasingly angry, while trying not to let the rest of his guests be aware that anything is amiss.)

He shall be endur'd

What, goodman boy, I say, he shall, go to!

Am I the master here, or you? go to!

You'll not endure him? God shall mend my soul,

You'll make a mutiny among my guests!

You will set cock-a-hoop! you'll be the man!

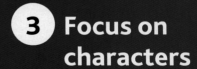

# Focus on characters

## Learning objective

- To develop the skill of discussing characters and their relationships

A play would not be a play without characters. Even if you are writing about a play's events or themes, you will need to write about the characters too. You are now going to think in detail about the characters from the Shakespeare play you are studying.

**Activity 1**

Make notes on the main character(s) in the Shakespeare play you are studying, using these prompts:

- the first time the character is mentioned in the play – what impressions would an audience receive of him or her?
- the first words spoken by the character – would these support or contradict an audience's earliest impressions?
- the five or six most important parts of the play for your character
- your character's most important relationships, and how they change in the course of the play
- a key quotation for your character
- the last time your character appears or is mentioned – what impressions would an audience receive of him or her this time?
- three words to describe your chosen character
- a one-sentence summary of your character's role.

An example is shown opposite.

**Stretch**

Prepare similar notes on some of the minor characters in the play you are studying.

**Activity 2**

Imagine that a friend who doesn't know the play as well as you do has been chosen to play a major role in the Shakespeare play you are studying. They have asked for your advice.

a. Write down what you would say, maybe using the framework opposite as a guide.

b. You could do this activity orally in pairs too.

| Focus on Emilia, from *Othello* | |
|---|---|
| **First mentioned/ seen** | • when Iago in soliloquy says he suspects she has been unfaithful, although he says he knows 'not if 't be true.' Audience would feel sympathy for her?<br>• then seen arriving in Cyprus, as Desdemona's servant, and is kissed by Cassio |
| **First words spoken** | • joking (probably?) with Iago when he is giving his sexist views on women. She seems to give as good as she gets ('You have little cause to say so.')<br>• audience may admire her attitude, or could feel sorry for her as Iago seems to pay more attention to Desdemona |
| **Key parts of play** | • helps Cassio gain access to Desdemona<br>• steals Desdemona's handkerchief in an attempt to please Iago<br>• unwittingly describes her husband, to his face, as 'most villainous' for having misled Othello<br>• bedchamber scene with Desdemona; her views on marriage<br>• killed by Iago when she tells Othello the truth |
| **Most important relationships** | • with Iago and with Desdemona<br>• loyal to Desdemona throughout, increasingly suspicious of Iago, although she wants to please him at the start (because she loves him, or because she is scared of him?) |
| **Key quotation** | • 'I will speak as liberal as the north' |
| **Last time seen/ mentioned** | • killed by Iago ('So speaking as I think, I die.')<br>• audience admire her for her loyalty and bravery, and sympathize with her for how her husband treats her |
| **In three words** | • gutsy, loyal, passionate |
| **In a sentence** | • yet another victim of Iago's manipulation, who dies for telling the truth. |

# 4 Exploring the themes

## Learning objective

- To learn to identify and discuss themes in Shakespeare

**Themes** such as love, war and ambition are the big ideas in a play. The Shakespeare play you have studied will probably include more than one main theme, and may also include other, minor, themes. Here you will look closely at the themes of the play you have studied, and identify where and how they are shown in the play.

### Activity 1

a. With a partner, or in a small group, brainstorm as many themes as you can think of in the Shakespeare play you have studied.

b. Sort your themes into order of importance, with the most important at the top.

### Activity 2

You are going to focus on one of the themes and make a poster about it.

a. Write the name of the theme in the middle of the poster, and then around it add:

- examples of where the theme is developed and explored
- brief details of which characters are involved, and what is happening.

Below is an example of how this might look for the theme of leadership in *Henry V*.

b. Choose brief quotations for each part of the play you have highlighted, and explain what they show about the theme. You could add these to your poster, if you like.

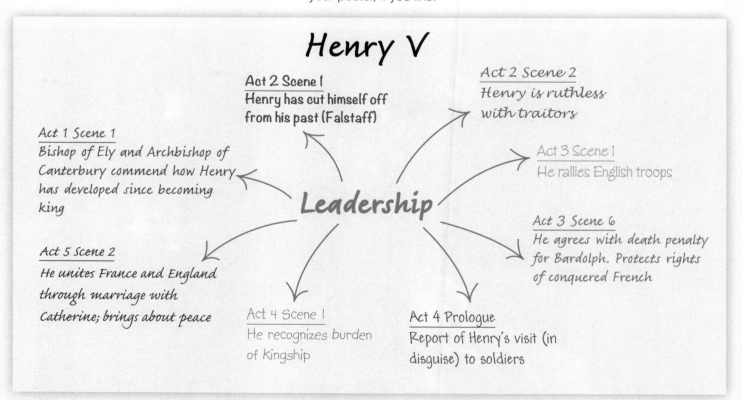

**Henry V**

Act 2 Scene 1
Henry has cut himself off from his past (Falstaff)

Act 2 Scene 2
Henry is ruthless with traitors

Act 1 Scene 1
Bishop of Ely and Archbishop of Canterbury commend how Henry has developed since becoming king

Act 3 Scene 1
He rallies English troops

**Leadership**

Act 3 Scene 6
He agrees with death penalty for Bardolph. Protects rights of conquered French

Act 5 Scene 2
He unites France and England through marriage with Catherine; brings about peace

Act 4 Scene 1
He recognizes burden of Kingship

Act 4 Prologue
Report of Henry's visit (in disguise) to soldiers

## Activity 3

The themes of a play are shown through events and through characters. Choose another theme from the play you have studied and break down how and where the theme is most obvious in the play, by creating a poster organized under the following headings:

- When?
- Who?
- How?

Add supporting quotations to back up the different parts of your poster, as in the example below, which shows some possible notes for a poster on friendship in *The Merchant of Venice*.

Other friendships in *The Merchant of Venice* could include Portia and Nerissa, Gratiano and Bassanio, and Jessica and Lancelot.

**Exam link**

Be sure to cover the whole of the play when you are writing about it – beginning, middle *and* end.

**Tip** The rule with quotations is: the shorter the better, but make sure you include enough of them to make sense!

### Friendship in The Merchant of Venice

**When?** Act 1 Scene 1; Act 2 Scene 8; Act 3 Scene 2; Act 4 Scene 1; Act 5 Scene 1

**Who?** Antonio and Bassanio

**How?** Points with brief quotations include:

**1** Antonio cares so much about Bassanio's happiness that he immediately offers to use his credit to go and court Portia, by entering into the risky deal with Shylock: 'have it of my trust or for my sake.'

**2** Solanio and Salarino gossiping about them: 'I think he only loves the world for him.'

**3** Bassanio's reaction to the letter from Antonio:
'...Here is a letter, lady,
The paper as the body of my friend,
And every word in it a gaping wound
Issuing lifeblood.'

**4** In the trial scene, where Antonio is prepared to die for Bassanio:
'Give me your hand, Bassanio. Fare you well.
Grieve not that I am fall'n to this for you.'

**5** Bassanio introduces Antonio to Portia:
'This is the man, this is Antonio,
To whom I am so infinitely bound.'

# 5 Focus on mood and atmosphere

## Learning objective

- To develop understanding of how mood and atmosphere are created in Shakespeare's plays

Shakespeare, like any playwright, had to work hard to keep his audience interested throughout his plays. In fact, he probably had to work even harder because he could not rely on lighting and special effects, as modern playwrights can. One way he did this was by controlling and changing the mood and atmosphere. One scene might produce laughter, tension, shock, horror and relief, all at different times.

## Activity 1

a. Choose a scene from the Shakespeare play you have studied.

b. Track how and why its mood and atmosphere change, and the impact this would have on an audience. The table below, for example, tracks a scene from *Much Ado About Nothing* for its changing mood and atmosphere.

### Key term

**Empathy:** really understanding a character, 'getting under their skin' and feeling for them. The verb is 'to empathize', so here, an audience may *empathize* with the character of Hero or *have empathy* for her

| | *Much Ado About Nothing*, Act 4 Scene 1 | |
|---|---|---|
| | **What's happening** | **Mood and atmosphere/effect on audience** |
| 1 | Characters gather for wedding between Hero and Claudio. | Tension – audience knows about Don John's plot |
| 2 | Claudio says he will not marry Hero as she is not a virgin. | Shock at Claudio's harshness |
| 3 | Hero is bewildered. | **Empathy** for Hero's confusion and distress |
| 4 | Don Pedro defends Claudio. | Disappointment in Don Pedro siding with Claudio |
| 5 | Hero faints. | Shock at the dramatic faint |
| 6 | Leonato takes against his daughter too. | Sympathy for Hero's increasing isolation |
| 7 | The Friar tries to defend Hero. | Relief that the Friar, at least, is still on Hero's side |
| 8 | Benedick starts to suspect Don John. | More relief that Benedick may not be so easily deceived |
| 9 | The Friar's plan: to pretend that Hero has died. | Intrigue at the Friar's plan, and suspense about whether it will work |
| 10 | Beatrice and Benedick are left alone and declare their love for one another. | Support for Beatrice and admiration for her strength and loyalty |
| 11 | Beatrice demands that Benedick should kill Claudio. | Shock (or maybe amusement, or nervous laughter?) at her demand |
| 12 | Benedick says he will challenge Claudio to a duel. | Tension/suspense racked up again. What will happen next? |

**Support**

You may find it helpful to show a scene's changing mood and atmosphere in the form of a graph.

**Stretch**

Can you pinpoint key lines in your chosen section where the mood and atmosphere you have identified are at their height? For example, 'Kill Claudio' in the table opposite might have an audience gasping in shock or giggling nervously.

**Progress check**

### Quickfire responses

Now you should be fully confident in your knowledge and understanding of the Shakespeare play you have studied, so use the questions below as a guide to check that this is the case. Answer each question with the first (sensible!) idea that comes into your head. Once you have done so, make sure that you can support your initial response with a reason, or reasons. You may do this task on your own, with a partner, or in a small group.

a. For which character do you have the most sympathy?

b. For which character do you have the least sympathy?

c. Which character changes most during the course of the play?

d. Which relationship between characters is the most important in the play?

e. Identify the most important turning point in the play.

f. Identify a part of the play that an audience would find funny.

g. Identify a part of the play where an audience might be shocked.

h. Identify a part of the play where an audience might be saddened.

i. What do you think are the three most important themes of the play?

j. What would be the main reaction of an audience at the end of the play?

 **Tip** As long as your answer is sensible, and you can support it with good reasons and evidence from the play, you can't be wrong. If you are working in a pair or group, be prepared to defend your point of view!

# **2** Poetry Anthology

## Assessment Objectives

In this part of the exam, you will be assessed against these Assessment Objectives:

- **AO1** Read, understand and respond to the texts, maintaining a critical style, developing a personal response, and using textual references, including quotations, to support and illustrate interpretations

- **AO2** Analyse the language, form and structure used by writers to create meanings and effects, using relevant subject terminology where appropriate

- **AO3** Show understanding of the relationships between texts and the contexts in which they were written

In this section of the book, you will develop the skills needed for writing about poems from the Poetry Anthology you are studying. You will get plenty of practice in developing the skills necessary to tackle the exam questions, by showing an understanding of:

- **what the poems are about**

- **the themes, or key ideas, of the poems**

- **the way the poems are written and organized (the structure)**

- **the relationships between the poems and the contexts in which they were written.**

 **Tip** If you feel confident in your knowledge of all the poems, it will be easier for you to make a good choice of second poem.

# In the exam

You will need to show your close-reading skills by discussing in detail two poems from the Anthology, one of which will be supplied as part of the exam paper. You will also need to make some comparisons between them.

You will look closely at the printed Anthology poem, then choose another, which has some similarities, and answer a question on each one.

There will be two questions.

- The first will focus on the printed poem. There will be guidelines about what you may write about, such as its theme.

- The second will ask you to choose a second poem from the Anthology, linked in some way to the first. There will be similar guidelines for your response, but you will not have a copy of this poem in the exam with you. You will then write about the second poem, in order to compare your chosen poem with the printed one.

While it is important to explain clearly how you think the poems are similar and different, your first, and most important, job is to show your understanding of and response to each poem.

## Context

This could include reference to the poet's background, if it has relevance to the poem and the way it is written. However, it may also apply to:

- when and where the poem is set

- the type of poem it is (a sonnet, for example)

- how different audiences may respond to it.

## A word about comparing

When you are comparing two poems, you will find it helpful to use some of the following words or phrases:

- 'on the other hand'

- 'whereas'

- 'however'

- 'but'

- 'similarly'

- 'also'.

You may find similarities or differences in:

- the themes of the poems

- their content; what they are about

- their tone

- the way they are written, including language and structure.

# 'The Manhunt' by Simon Armitage

## Learning objectives

- To understand the key ideas of the poem, by tracking through its detail
- To form an overview of the poem's content, themes, the way it is written, and its context

**Tip** When quoting from a poem, it's best to keep your quotations brief – the shorter the better. Using embedded quotations (just a word or two within your sentences) is a good skill to develop. For example: 'Comparing his lung to "parachute silk" makes it sound beautiful, delicate and vulnerable.'

### Activity 1

**First impressions**

Read the poem, pausing at each punctuation mark, so that you work out what is going on – the story of the poem.

**a.** What impressions do you get of the speaker in the poem, and of their relationship with the wounded man?

**b.** What are the feelings of the speaker?

**c.** What do you make of the last six lines of the poem?

### Activity 2

**Looking at the detail**

A lot of **images** are used here. The man's scar on his face is described as 'the frozen river' and his lower jaw as a 'blown hinge.'

**a.** How might these images be effective?

**b.** What about 'porcelain collar-bone' and 'parachute silk of his punctured lung'? What qualities do porcelain and silk have in common? How might this relate to the meaning of the poem?

**c.** The person describes how they have to 'climb the rungs of his broken ribs.' What does this suggest about their feelings and movements?

**d.** How might the man's heart be 'grazed'?

**e.** The bullet is described as a 'foetus of metal.' What could this imply?

**f.** What might the 'sweating, unexploded mine/buried deep in his mind' refer to?

**g.** Now you have thought about the poem in detail, what is the significance of the title?

### Activity 3

**Structure**

As you read this poem, you may have noticed how at the start the rhyme scheme is regular, but it becomes more broken and less organized as the poem progresses.

**a.** How might this add to the overall meaning of the poem?

**b.** The phrase 'only then' is repeated four times in the poem. What could be the effect of this?

**c.** The poem ends abruptly. What do you think of this?

## Activity 4

### Themes

There are several possible themes in this poem: war and its effects; relationships; love; suffering, both mental and physical. Which one do you think is the most important, and why?

## Activity 5

### Context

This poem is personal, but also universal, which means it could apply to a single situation and a specific couple affected by a war, or to anyone affected by any war.

It was written for a documentary about how soldiers are affected by war and injury and was read in the programme by Laura Beddoes. Her husband, Eddie Beddoes, was one of the peacekeeping task force in Bosnia in the 1990s and was discharged because of injury and depression.

How may this specific background make the poem more effective? Give reasons for what you say.

### Support

When you have read the whole poem, make a list of the injuries the man has suffered. Compare your list with that of someone else in your class. Are they the same?

### Stretch

Thinking of the poem as a whole, how effective do you find the title? Can you think of any other titles that might have been effective?

# 'Sonnet 43' by Elizabeth Barrett Browning

## Learning objectives

- To understand the key ideas of the poem, by tracking through its detail
- To form an overview of the poem's content, themes, the way it is written, and its context

### Key terms

**Caesura:** a clear pause, right in the middle of a line

**Sonnet:** a traditional poetic form with 14 lines, often split into two parts. It traditionally uses the rhythm of **iambic pentameter**

**Iambic pentameter:** ten syllables or 'beats' to each line, with the pattern of 'te-dum'; it is the rhythm pattern closest to the rhythm of spoken English, so poets often use it to create a conversational tone. It sounds like a steady heartbeat (te-dum; te-dum; te-dum; te-dum; te-dum). For example: 'Most **qui**et **need**, by **sun** and **can**dle**light**.'

 **Activity 1**

### First impressions

**a.** As you read the poem, jot down what you think the main message is, and what you think about it.

**b.** What sort of person is speaking? A teenager in love for the first time, or someone more mature? Find evidence for what you decide. Look particularly closely at the last six lines to help you here.

 **Activity 2**

### Looking at the detail

**a.** What tone is set up in the first line, 'How do I love thee? Let me count the ways.' What is the effect of the **caesura** and the direct address?

**b.** The rest of the poem lists the different ways the speaker loves someone. Count the number of times the words 'love' and 'I love thee' are used. What is the effect of this repetition?

**c.** What is suggested by the contrast of 'by sun and candlelight'?

 **Activity 3**

### Structure

This poem is a **sonnet**, and follows the rules of a sonnet in its structure. Why may this be effective, bearing in mind its content and message?

**Activity 4**

### Themes

The obvious theme here is love. Can you think of any other relevant themes here? Relationships? Ageing?

**Activity 5**

### Context

In all probability, Elizabeth Barrett Browning wrote this sonnet for her husband, Robert, who was also a poet, whom she had met and eloped with in later life. However, as no gender or name is mentioned here, you may think that this gives the poem a universal quality. Do you find it helps your understanding of this poem to know something of the poet's life?

## Activity 6

Try writing a few lines of a love poem (or you could write a whole sonnet, if you like!) in **iambic pentameter**. You could start similarly to Elizabeth Barrett Browning, but you may wish to update the language and ideas.

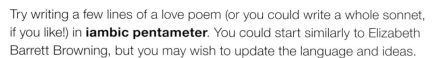

'How do I love you? Let me count the ways...'

### Support

This poem is often read at weddings. Practise reading it aloud, as if in front of an audience. You may also choose suitable music to play in the background.

### Stretch

Carry out some research into Elizabeth Barrett Browning and her relationship with her husband, Robert Browning. How does this knowledge affect your interpretation of the sonnet?

# 'London' by William Blake

## Learning objectives

- To understand the key ideas of the poem, by tracking through its detail
- To form an overview of the poem's content, themes, the way it is written, and its context

## Key terms

**Image / imagery:** pictures in words. They may include similes or metaphors

**Stanza:** another word for a verse in poetry

**Iambic tetrameter:** eight-syllable line, with the rhythm 'te-dum'

**Romantic movement:** the Romantic poets were writing in the late 18th and early 19th centuries. Their main concern was to make poetry accessible to as many people as possible. Some other qualities were their love of nature and dislike of urban life, an interest in the supernatural and mystical, and in ordinary people

**Tip**

To work out the syllable pattern, it may be helpful to read a line (or lines) aloud, while marking out the syllables with the fingers of one hand, almost as if you are playing the piano.

### Activity 1

#### First impressions

a. Although this poem is only 16 lines long, it is dense with **imagery**. As you read it, jot down what you think the speaker's feelings are.

b. What is the effect of the image of the poet or speaker as someone walking through London, as an observer?

c. Make a note of the images of the city and what overall impression of London you think these images create.

### Activity 2

#### Looking at the detail

a. Considering there are only 26 words in the first **stanza**, there is a lot of repetition. What do you think of the repetition of 'charter'd' and 'mark'?

b. There is a lot of negative imagery in each stanza. Make a list of the negative words or images. What do they have in common? You may notice how there is a general atmosphere of disease and seediness, as well as of being constricted or imprisoned.

c. What about the people mentioned in the poem? What do they have in common? What impressions of society do they give?

### Activity 3

#### Structure

a. The poem is written with a strict rhythm and rhyme. If you count out the syllables as you read it, you will notice that it starts with eight beats to a line, with the 'te-dum' rhythm of the iambic beat. This is called **iambic tetrameter**.

   'I **wan**der **thro'** each **char**ter'd **street**.'

   Sometimes it switches to seven syllables, however. What effect does this create?

b. The rhyme scheme is also regular. What impressions does this give?

## Activity 4

### Themes

There are plenty of themes in this poem, such as freedom and imprisonment, death, the abuse of power, and childhood. Maybe you can think of more. Which of these themes do you think are the most important? Give reasons for what you say.

## Activity 5

### Context

a. The poem was published as part of William Blake's *Songs of Innocence and Experience*, just after the French Revolution in the late 18th century, a time of political upheaval. What points do you think Blake wanted to put across?

b. Blake was part of the **Romantic movement**, and the poem's apparent simplicity and concern with personal experience are typical of the Romantic literary tradition. Although this poem appears to be written about a specific time and place, do you think it could be considered relevant to different places in the world at different times in history – even the 21st century? Give reasons for what you say.

### Support

Working in a group, prepare a reading of this poem as a performance that will make its meaning and messages clear.

### Stretch

Create a poster for this poem, illustrating its key images, so that the main messages of the poem come across clearly.

# 'The Soldier' by Rupert Brooke

## Learning objectives

- To understand the key ideas of the poem, by tracking through its detail
- To form an overview of the poem's content, themes, the way it is written, and its context

### Key terms

**Caesura:** a clear pause, right in the middle of a line

**Petrarchan sonnet:** a sonnet that is divided into two parts, of eight and six lines; it is named after the Italian poet Petrarch

**Octave / octet:** eight lines of poetry, often the first part of a sonnet

**Sestet:** six lines of poetry, often the second part of a sonnet

**Stanza:** another word for a verse in poetry

**Iambic pentameter:** ten syllables or 'beats' to each line, with the pattern 'te-dum'; it is the rhythm pattern closest to the rhythm of spoken English

**Enjambement:** where the sense of a line carries on from one line to the next, without a pause

 **Activity 1**

### First impressions

**a.** Read the poem, taking note of the punctuation, so that the meaning comes across. That, together with the title, will get you a long way in understanding this poem.

**b.** What are your feelings about this poem? Do you find it moving? Naive? Idealistic? Sentimental? Patriotic? Comforting? Give reasons for what you say.

**Activity 2**

### Looking at the detail

**a.** The opening line is quite abrupt in tone. What effect does this have?

**b.** Look at the full stop after 'England', which creates a **caesura**, and then count the references to England or English in the poem as a whole. What is the effect of this repetition and of the break after the first mention of England?

**c.** What impressions of England do you get from reading this poem? Give reasons for what you say.

**d.** What is implied by 'In that rich earth a richer dust concealed'?

 **Activity 3**

### Structure

**a.** This is a **Petrarchan sonnet**, divided into a clear **octet** and **sestet**. What are the key ideas in each **stanza** of the poem?

**b.** The regular rhythm of the **iambic pentameter** and the use of **enjambement** create a conversational tone. What impact might that have on you as a reader?

**Activity 4**

### Themes

The most obvious themes are probably death and war, but there is also patriotism, and being connected to the natural world.

Try putting these themes in rank order, and be prepared to defend your decisions.

## Activity 5

### Context

**a.** What is the effect of using the traditional sonnet form for this poem? What might it suggest about the poet's/speaker's feelings?

**b.** It's important to be aware that Rupert Brooke wrote this poem before the First World War had actually started, in 1914. He died in 1915, from blood poisoning, while serving in the Royal Navy (so, ironically, he was buried in 'some corner of a foreign field', in Skyros, in Greece). We know now of the horrific nature and huge numbers of deaths in the First World War, but what impressions of death in war are given here? Do you think this affects its impact, or, perhaps, may add to it?

### Support

Carry out some research into Rupert Brooke's life and death. Prepare a brief talk on what you found out.

### Stretch

Discuss with a partner, or in a group, whether you think Brooke really believed in the sentiments in this poem, and what alternative interpretations may be possible.

# 'She Walks in Beauty' by Lord Byron

## Learning objectives

- To understand the key ideas of the poem, by tracking through its detail
- To form an overview of the poem's content, themes, the way it is written, and its context

### Key terms

**Image / imagery:** pictures in words. They may include similes or metaphors

**Stanza:** another word for a verse in poetry

**Alliteration:** repetition of initial consonants for a specific effect

**Iambic tetrameter:** eight-syllable line, with the rhythm 'te-dum'

**Universal quality:** something that can apply to anyone, at any time or place

## Activity 1

### First impressions

a. If possible, read this poem aloud, and notice what effect this has – it's almost like a song, with its regular rhythm and rhyme.

b. What do you think of the speaker in the poem? In love? Infatuated? Obsessed? Romantic?

c. And what impressions do you get of the woman being described? Attractive? Graceful? Lively? Extroverted? Calm? Thoughtful?

d. There are quite a few clues as to her physical appearance. Could you describe her? Remember to be prepared to give reasons for what you say.

## Activity 2

### Looking at the detail

a. What do you make of the first four lines? Everything seems perfect, as well as beautiful. Too perfect, perhaps?

b. Look at the **imagery** of balance here, for example, 'One shade the more, one ray the less.' What effect does this have?

c. It is quite unusual to use night as an image of beauty in a love poem. Why might Byron have chosen to do this?

d. 'Dear' in the final line of the first **stanza** could be a play on words. What are the two possible meanings of 'dear'? How may they fit in with the meaning of the poem here?

e. There is quite a lot of **alliteration** in this poem. How does it add to the overall effect?

f. What do you think the last line, 'A heart whose love is innocent' suggests? Remember to be prepared to give reasons for what you say.

## Activity 3

### Structure

a. Count the syllables in each line. It's a regular pattern (**iambic tetrameters**) and the rhyme scheme follows a strict pattern too. How does this affect the effect of the poem and its meaning, in your opinion?

b. What about the stanzas? Do you think the ideas develop, or does each part just add to the overall impression of both the speaker and the woman he is describing?

## Activity 4

### Themes

What do you think are the important themes here? Love? Male/female relationships? Appearances? Something else? Remember, as long as you can support what you say, you can't really be wrong when writing about poetry.

## Activity 5

### Context

a. Although Lord Byron died when he was only 36, he led a very eventful life, including romantically. Do you think this knowledge affects your reading of the poem (some people think it's written about a specific person) or does it have more of a **universal quality**?

b. Although this appears to be a love poem, the word 'love' is never mentioned. Do you think this makes a difference?

c. There is evidence that Byron's writing here is part of the Romantic tradition, in the way it contains the idea of heart over head, the references to the natural world, and the suggestion that nature represents innocence and purity. Make a list of features from the poem that suggest it is in the Romantic tradition.

### Support

With a partner, read the poem as if you were the speaker talking to a friend, then swap around. What might be the response and reactions of the listener?

### Stretch

Find out about Byron and his relationships with women. In the light of this knowledge, are you surprised by the tone of this poem?

# 'Living Space' by Imtiaz Dharker

## Learning objectives

- To understand the key ideas of the poem, by tracking through its detail
- To form an overview of the poem's content, themes, the way it is written, and its context

### Key terms

**Tone:** the feeling behind what is written. It could be calm, angry, shocked or surprised, for example

**Stanza:** another word for a verse in poetry

**Pace:** the speed at which the text or part of a text is read – it may be quick, slow, or steady, for example

**Enjambement:** where the sense of a line carries on from one line to the next, without a pause

## Activity 1

### First impressions

a. Read the poem straight through, following the punctuation marks as a guide, and quickly write down all your impressions from this first reading.

b. What is the **tone** of the first **stanza**? Confusion? Bemusement? Amazement?

c. What sort of place is being described?

d. The whole of the last stanza focuses on the eggs in the wire basket. What impressions do you get here?

## Activity 2

### Looking at the detail

a. The general impression in the first stanza, in particular, is one of chaos and being constricted. Which words and phrases create this impression?

b. What do these images of chaos suggest about the society in which this place exists?

c. Notice how the word 'miraculous' at the end of the first stanza leads you into the rest of the poem. What impact does this have on the poem?

d. The word 'someone' is the first mention of a person. What is the effect of this?

e. Why is there such a close focus on the eggs? Look at the words used to describe them and think about what eggs may represent – fragility? Hope for the future? Dreams, though easily shattered?

f. Do you find this poem optimistic or pessimistic in its portrayal of the society it describes?

## Activity 3

### Structure

a. The poem is clearly divided into three very different stanzas.

b. Count the sentences in the first stanza. As you read it, what is the effect of the way this stanza is laid out?

c. The rest of the poem is all one sentence. How does this affect the **pace** of the poem? Think about the poet's use of **enjambement** here.

d. The middle stanza makes a focal point of the 'living space' featured in the title. Why might the poet have made this stanza so short?

e. The final stanza focuses on the eggs. How does this change the tone of the whole poem?

## Activity 4

### Themes

What are the important themes in this poem? Society? Survival? Hopes and dreams? Give reasons for what you say.

## Activity 5

### Context

Imtiaz Dharker has said that this poem is set in Mumbai (formerly called Bombay) in India, although no place is mentioned in the poem. Does this make a difference to how you interpret it? Could this poem apply equally to any impoverished society?

### Support

Find some pictures of Mumbai or of another city that would support the impressions you get from this poem. Explain how they connect to your reading of the poem.

### Stretch

Imtiaz Dharker is an artist as well as a poet. Imagine that she is going to create a work of art to represent this poem. Working in a group, decide what the key idea/s and images are in the poem, and how she might illustrate and present them.

# 'As Imperceptibly As Grief' by Emily Dickinson

## Learning objectives

- To understand the key ideas of the poem, by tracking through its detail
- To form an overview of the poem's content, themes, the way it is written, and its context

## Key terms

**Sibilance:** a sort of hissing sound, created by repeating 's' or 'sh' sounds

**Personification:** making something not alive sound as if it is alive

**Stanza:** another word for a verse in poetry

**Half-rhyme:** exactly what it sounds like: nearly a rhyme, but not quite, like 'keel' and 'beautiful'

**Alliteration:** repetition of initial consonants for a specific effect

### Activity 1

### First impressions

As you read through this poem for the first time (aloud, if possible), don't worry about understanding every single word, but focus instead on how it sounds.

You will discover that there is a lot of **sibilance** (soft sounds) and this, together with the relatively difficult words, makes it tricky to read at first. Both these things combine to make it sound soft and gentle – maybe like someone whispering. This, together with the word 'grief' in the title, should begin to give you some ideas about what the poem is about.

### Activity 2

### Looking at the detail

a. Use a dictionary, if necessary, to check on some of the less common words here, such as 'imperceptible', 'Perfidy', 'distilled', 'Sequestered' and 'harrowing'. Combine these with the words you're more familiar with – what general feeling do you have for the poem now? Does it fit in with your initial impressions?

b. The poem on the surface seems to be about summer changing into autumn, but at a deeper level it could be about grief at someone leaving, perhaps dying. Can you find any evidence to support this interpretation?

c. What is the significance of the **personification** of 'Nature'?

d. Why do you think the morning is described as 'foreign'?

e. What do you make of the final four lines? Does this affect your interpretation of the poem as a whole?

### Activity 3

### Structure

The poem looks simple and straightforward on the page, with four equal **stanzas** and **half-rhymes** on every other line. Why do you think the poet decided on this structure?

You can't help but notice that Dickinson uses capital letters for important words (usually, but not always, nouns). She did this in all her poems. You may think it creates a sense of 'otherness'. Or can you think of any other reasons why she might have done this?

## Activity ④

### Themes

Although this is quite a simple poem, there are several themes within it: change, death, grief, nature, regret and acceptance, for example. Which do you think are the most important, and why?

## Activity ⑤

### Context

**a.** Emily Dickinson was an American poet who lived in the 19th century. She was known to be reclusive and quiet. How might this knowledge add to your appreciation of the poem?

**b.** Would you classify the poem as a poem about love, loss, or nature? Or is it about all these things and maybe more?

**c.** The poem follows quite a traditional form, although Dickinson's use of subtle half-rhymes and the sibilance (**alliteration** of the letter 's') helps contribute to its effect for a modern reader. Do you think this poem is as effective for a reader in the 21st century as it would have been in the 19th century, when it was written?

Always remember to give reasons for what you say.

### Support

This poem has particularly complicated words in it. Try paraphrasing it (putting it in your own words). What is lost or gained?

### Stretch

Read some more poems by Emily Dickinson. What do you find they seem to have in common?

# 'Cozy Apologia' by Rita Dove

## Learning objectives

- To understand the key ideas of the poem, by tracking through its detail

- To form an overview of the poem's content, themes, the way it is written, and its context

### Key terms

**Stanza:** another word for a verse in poetry

**Image / imagery:** pictures in words. They may include similes or metaphors

**First person:** the speaker's point of view, shown by words like 'I', 'me', 'we', 'us'

**Second person:** the person the speaker is addressing, shown by the word 'you'

**Colloquial:** in an informal style, with language that is used in everyday conversation

**Proper nouns:** real names of people, places or things

**Enjambement:** where the sense of a line carries on from one line to the next, without a pause

### Activity 1

#### First impressions

**a.** Read the poem as if you were reading a story, going from punctuation mark to punctuation mark, and see if you can work out the 'story' of this poem.

**b.** Read the poem again, and try to answer the following questions:
- What do you find out about the speaker?
- The poem is dedicated to 'Fred'. What impressions do you get of him from your reading of the poem?
- What are the writer's feelings at the end of the poem?

### Activity 2

#### Looking at the detail

**a.** Look at how the poet describes her partner in the first **stanza**. What **imagery** does she use, and what does this suggest about their relationship?

**b.** What is the writer's attitude towards her life of work and her past?

**c.** At the end of the poem we realize that the couple are in the same house, both working. What do you learn about their relationship here?

**d.** The poet writes in the **first person**, addressing someone in the **second person**. What effect does this have on the poem?

**e.** What do you make of the title? 'Apologia' means a defence of one's options or actions, and 'cozy' is the American spelling of 'cosy.'

**f.** What do you make of the tone of the poem? Is it witty? Romantic? Realistic? Down to earth?

Always remember to give reasons for what you say.

### Activity 3

#### Structure

The poem is written in a **colloquial**, straightforward and conversational style. What in the way it is structured or organized creates this effect? Think about the sort of words that are used, the use of **proper nouns** and the use of **enjambement**, for example. It may appear very informal, but have a closer look at the rhyme scheme. It is regular at first, but then changes. Can you identify how and why it changes, and the effect this has?

## Activity 4

### Themes

The more obvious theme here is love between established partners, and therefore relationships, but there is also nature (the effects of the hurricane on the writer) and the act of creation (presumably they're both writing).

Can you think of any others?

## Activity 5

### Context

This poem has a specific place and time, as the hurricane mentioned, 'Big Bad Floyd', occurred on the Atlantic coast of the USA in 1999. It's safe to assume, therefore, that the 'I' writing in this poem is Rita Dove herself, an African-American poet, and 'Fred' is her German husband.

Do you think this biographical information adds to or detracts from your enjoyment of the poem?

### Support

Choose your favourite quotations from the poem and explain why you chose them.

### Stretch

This poem can be seen as funny and witty. What in the way it is written may create this impression?

# 'Valentine' by Carol Ann Duffy

## Learning objectives

- To understand the key ideas of the poem, by tracking through its detail
- To form an overview of the poem's content, themes, the way it is written, and its context

### Key terms

**First person:** the speaker's point of view, shown by words like 'I', 'me', 'we', 'us'

**Metaphor:** a simile without the words 'like' or 'as'

**Image / imagery:** pictures in words. They may include similes or metaphors

**Enjambement:** where the sense of a line carries on from one line to the next, without a pause

**Contemporary:** living or happening at the same time as something else; up to date

**Tip** When you write about the techniques a poet has used, never just 'spot' stylistic features (for example, 'The poet uses a metaphor') without explaining how the technique helps to convey the messages of the poem.

## Activity 1

### First impressions

a. With a partner, read the poem straight through to one another, then compare notes on how it felt to have someone say that to you.

b. Most people would prefer a more conventional gift to an onion! What are your first thoughts on why Duffy chose this shock opening?

c. Jot down your initial ideas about onions. Can you see anything they may have in common with love?

d. What impact do you think this poem may have? Do you think the poet set out to shock with this poem?

e. Carol Ann Duffy says that she likes to use simple words in a complicated way. Do you think that is what she has done here?

## Activity 2

### Looking at the detail

a. The poem is written in the **first person**, as if addressing the speaker's lover, in the present tense. It uses straightforward language. What is the effect of this?

b. What do you think is the tone of the poem? Does it change at all? If so, why and how? You may think it is direct, confident, maybe with a note of warning at the end – or something else.

c. The image of love as an onion in this poem is an extended **metaphor**. Look at the phrases and **images** below, and think about how they are effective here.

- 'a moon wrapped in brown paper'
- 'It promises light'
- 'the careful undressing of love'
- 'It will blind you with tears'
- 'like a lover.'
- 'Its fierce kiss will stay on your lips'
- 'Its platinum loops shrink to a wedding-ring'

d. What do you think of the ending of the poem? What might the knife symbolize?

## Activity 3

### Structure

The form or structure of the poem is very irregular. When you read it aloud, did you find you read it in a rather jerky, uneven way? What in the way it is structured may cause this effect?

Look at the use of **enjambement**, the short sentences and the very short lines, sometimes only one word. What effects do you think these have?

## Activity 4

### Themes

The title may make this sound like a conventional love poem. Do you think its theme is love? What other themes might there be? Relationships? Trust? Betrayal?

## Activity 5

### Context

a. 'Valentine' is a **contemporary** poem, written in the early 1990s. If you had not known this, what clues might tell you this?

b. Would you describe it as a contemporary love poem? Give reasons for what you say.

c. In Duffy's poems, she often adopts the persona of another person. Do you think this may be the case here? Give reasons for what you say.

**Support**

With a partner, make a list of the different types of cards or presents you have heard of being given on Valentine's Day. Talk about how you would feel if you were given an onion.

**Stretch**

Find a more traditional love poem, either from the Anthology, or from your wider reading, and compare them side by side. Make a list of what they have in common and how they are different.

# 'A Wife in London' by Thomas Hardy

## Learning objectives

- To understand the key ideas of the poem, by tracking through its detail
- To form an overview of the poem's content, themes, the way it is written, and its context

### Key terms

**Stanza:** another word for a verse in poetry

**Pathetic fallacy:** where the weather, or nature, suggests the mood or feelings of characters

**Euphemism:** a way of saying something unpleasant in a nicer, often gentler, way

**Universal quality:** something that can apply to anyone, at any time or place

**Tip** To appreciate the mood and atmosphere of a poem, think about the colours or music that they suggest to you as you read it.

### Activity 1

#### First impressions

a. Read through the poem, working out the story by reading from punctuation mark to punctuation mark.

b. The storyline may not be immediately obvious, and you may want to check the meaning of some unfamiliar words, but the mood and atmosphere, or the feelings behind the story, probably are, so focus on these from the start.

c. If you were making a film of this poem, what sort of colours would you use? What sort of music would you have in the background?

d. Can you sum up the story of this poem in a sentence or two?

### Activity 2

#### Looking at the detail

a. What are the mood and atmosphere in the first **stanza**? How do you know?

b. Who do you think is the 'she' mentioned in the first line?

c. The poet uses **pathetic fallacy** here. How does the miserable, foggy weather suggest the feelings inside the house?

d. What are the mood and atmosphere in the second stanza? Have they changed at all? How? What has happened? What words stand out in this stanza and how are they effective?

e. The expression 'has fallen' is a **euphemism** for 'has died.' Why do you think this was used?

f. What about the expression 'the far South Land'? Why use this instead of something more specific?

g. The third stanza is set the next day. What happens here?

h. What do you think of the reference to 'the worm' and the way this leads into the final stanza, with the colon? What impact might this have on the reader?

i. The fourth stanza sums up the contents of the letter from the now-dead soldier. What has he said? What is your response to this as the ending of the poem? Some people think that the reference to 'new love' may refer to a baby or pregnancy. What do you think it may refer to?

## Activity 3

### Structure

a. The poem is made up of four even stanzas with a fairly regular rhythm and rhyme. Look at parts of the poem where the rhythm breaks, such as the final line of the second stanza. What effect does this have?

b. The poem divides into two parts. The first sets the situation and the second the aftermath. An item of correspondence features in each: the message (presumably a telegram) in the first, and the letter from the woman's dead husband in the second. How do you think this affects the mood and atmosphere?

c. Notice also how the weather changes in the last stanza. What is the effect of this, in your opinion?

d. Think about how and where Hardy has used contrast for effect in his poem.

## Activity 4

### Themes

There are a lot of possible themes in this poem: war, relationships, love, nature – and you may be able to think of more. Which do you think are the most important, and why?

## Activity 5

### Context

This poem was published at the end of the 19th century, in 1899, so the war mentioned was probably the Boer War, fought in South Africa. It is also clearly set in London, as indicated by the title and the reference to the River Thames.

Does this knowledge affect your interpretation of the poem, or do you think it could have a more **universal quality**? It would, of course, have been contemporary when it was first published. Do you think readers would have responded to it differently then? Give reasons for what you say.

**Support**

Imagine you are the woman in the poem. Write your diary for the days described.

**Stretch**

This poem is divided into two sections, each of two stanzas:

I   The Tragedy
II  The Irony

Do you think this adds to your appreciation of the poem?

# 'Death of a Naturalist' by Seamus Heaney

## Learning objectives

- To understand the key ideas of the poem, by tracking through its detail
- To form an overview of the poem's content, themes, the way it is written, and its context

### Key terms

**Stanza:** another word for a verse in poetry

**Simile:** a comparison or similarity between two things that aren't otherwise similar; it always contains the words 'like' or 'as'

**Metaphor:** a simile without the words 'like' or 'as'

**Onomatopoeia:** 'sound-effect' words – where the word sounds like what it describes

**Iambic pentameter:** ten syllables or 'beats' to each line, with the pattern 'te-dum'; it is the rhythm pattern closest to the rhythm of spoken English

**Enjambement:** where the sense of a line carries on from one line to the next, without a pause

**Caesura:** a clear pause, right in the middle of a line

**Colloquial language:** informal language such as that used in everyday conversation

## Activity 1

### First impressions

**a.** As you read through this poem, what impressions do you get of the place where it is set? What impressions do you get of the 'I' in the poem, who is presumably either the young Heaney, or someone very like him?

**b.** What impressions do you get of his school and childhood?

**c.** What is the effect of the change in the second **stanza**?

**d.** What do you think of the ending of the poem? What does it make you think of?

## Activity 2

### Looking at the detail

**a.** There are a lot of negative words and phrases right from the start. Make a note of them, and the general effect they have.

**b.** Choose what you think are some of the most effective **similes** and **metaphors**, and explain why you find them effective.

**c.** Heaney has used **onomatopoeia** throughout the poem. Find examples of this and explain what effects it achieves.

**d.** What is the effect of the childlike language in the poem? Find examples of childlike language to support what you say.

**e.** The poet appeals to most of the senses. Make a list of words or phrases where there is an appeal to the senses and see what senses are appealed to the most. How do you think this is effective?

**f.** What do you think of the title of the poem? Does it help you understand what it is about?

## Activity 3

### Structure

**a.** If you read this poem aloud, you will notice that it has a very conversational tone. That is partly because of the use of the **iambic pentameter**, partly because of the **enjambement** and use of **caesura**, and partly because of the **colloquial language**. Why do you think a conversational tone might be appropriate for the subject matter of the poem?

**b.** The poem is divided into two stanzas. What does each stanza deal with? How does this fit in with the content of the poem?

## Activity ④

### Themes

An obvious theme is growing up, but 'Death of a Naturalist' also deals with nature, the relationship between humans and nature, and change. Can you think of any others?

## Activity ⑤

### Context

Seamus Heaney grew up on a farm in rural Northern Ireland in the middle of the 20th century. A lot of his poems are based in this background. How does this knowledge affect your reading of the poem? Does it resonate with any of your own experiences?

> **Support**
>
> Write or talk about some of your childhood memories similar to those described here.

> **Stretch**
>
> Read some more of Heaney's poems about his childhood. Do they add to the impressions you gathered about him in 'Death of a Naturalist'?

# 'Hawk Roosting' by Ted Hughes

## Learning objectives

- To understand the key ideas of the poem, by tracking through its detail
- To form an overview of the poem's content, themes, the way it is written, and its context

### Activity

## First impressions

a. Read the poem, aloud if possible.

b. Whose 'voice' have you just been speaking in? Why do you think Ted Hughes chose to write this poem in this voice?

c. What sort of creature is the hawk, according to what he says about himself here?

d. What feelings do you have when you read the last line?

### Activity

## Looking at the detail

a. One of the most noticeable features of this poem is the number of **first-person** singular pronouns ('I', 'Me', 'My', 'Mine').

b. Count the number of first-person singular pronouns and, if you like, work that out as a proportion of the whole poem! What does this show you about the hawk's attitude?

c. Check how many of the words here are **monosyllabic** (having just one syllable). What effect does this have on the tone of the poem?

d. What is the mood or atmosphere here? Arrogant? Violent? Menacing? Threatening? Powerful? Proud? Hubristic (arrogantly proud)? Can you think of any more?

e. What words or images suggest the mood or atmosphere?

f. Having considered this, do you think the poem is just about a hawk, or might it apply to a certain type of person? What sort of person would you connect with this sort of attitude?

### Activity

## Structure

a. This poem is tightly organized into six four-line **stanzas**. How might this unchanging structure fit in with what the poem is about?

b. Look at the use of full stops in the poem. What effect do they have? How do they add to the tone?

c. Look at the words at the end of each line. Being at the end of a line always draws attention to a word. How does this contribute to the overall effect here?

## Activity 4

### Themes

There is a range of possible themes here, such as power, pride, nature, or the hubris of a dictator. With a partner, rank the possible themes in order of their importance. You will probably have to explain your choices – make sure you have reasons for what you say.

## Activity 5

### Context

Ted Hughes was a poet and writer of books for children in the 20th century. He was brought up in a small town in Yorkshire, and although he did not always live in the countryside, it often features in his poetry. Hughes frequently wrote about the dark side of nature in his poems. How do you think this appears in the poem 'Hawk Roosting'?

**Support**

Change the words in this poem to 'it' or 'he' instead of 'I'. In other words, write it in the third rather than the first person. What difference does this make to your understanding of the poem?

**Stretch**

Ted Hughes said that 'Hawk Roosting' is about a hawk, pure and simple, and that he had no intention of writing about any human characters. Do you think his original intention matters, or is how the poem could be interpreted more important?

**Tip** When writing about poetry, the key is to engage directly with the text, and work at what the detail suggests to you. Your ideas are just as valid as anyone else's, as long as you can back them up with evidence from the poem.

# 'To Autumn' by John Keats

## Learning objectives

- To understand the key ideas of the poem, by tracking through its detail
- To form an overview of the poem's content, themes, the way it is written, and its context

### Key terms

**Stanza:** another word for a verse in poetry

**Alliteration:** repetition of initial consonants for a specific effect

**Enjambement:** where the sense of a line carries on from one line to the next, without a pause

**Onomatopoeia:** 'sound-effect' words – where the word sounds like what it describes

**Personification (to personify):** making something not alive sound as if it is alive

**Ode:** a form of poetry with its roots in ancient Greece and Rome. In an ode, the poet addresses an object, or something that cannot answer back

**Iambic pentameter:** ten syllables or 'beats' to each line, with the pattern 'te-dum'; it is the rhythm pattern closest to the rhythm of spoken English

**Image / imagery:** pictures in words. They may include similes or metaphors

## Activity 1

### First impressions

a. The title of this poem gives a strong indication what it is about. As you read it, make notes on what impressions of autumn are given in each **stanza**.

b. In the first stanza, the focus is on the fruits of autumn. The overall impression is of plenty – what words and phrases give this effect? Notice that summer is mentioned in the final line. What stage of autumn is suggested in this stanza?

c. In the second stanza, the focus is on the harvest. What words and phrases here suggest that this stanza is about a later stage in autumn?

d. In the final stanza, what sights and sounds are described? What impressions of autumn are given here?

## Activity 2

### Looking at the detail

a. Read the poem again and, as you read, notice the use of **alliteration**, **enjambement**, **onomatopoeia** and repetition. Find examples of each, and consider what effects are achieved.

b. Keats appeals to the senses a lot in this poem. Find examples in every sentence where there is an appeal to the senses, and explain how each example you have chosen is effective.

c. What sort of character is Autumn **personified** as in the first two stanzas? How does this add to the overall impression of the season of autumn?

d. What are the mood and atmosphere in the final stanza? Some people may find it depressing because there are references to death, but others may see optimism here as there are hints of spring and the cycle of the year. Think about the significance of the swallows, for example. Find examples to support each point of view, and decide what your point of view is.

e. There are some rhetorical questions in the poem. What do you think their effect is? Although the poet is addressing autumn, do you think they help to connect the poet with the reader?

## Activity 3

### Structure

The poem, which is in the form of an **ode**, is structured in three separate stanzas. Although these are connected, each paints a distinctly different picture of autumn. Try to sum up in a sentence what each stanza is about.

The poem is written in **iambic pentameters**, which is the natural rhythm of spoken English and helps create a conversational tone. How does this add to the overall impact of the poem, in your opinion?

## Activity 4

### Themes

As with most poems, there is a range of themes here. Nature may be the most obvious one, but there are others: the relationship between nature and humans; the passing of time; change; mortality; acceptance. It could be said that the poem is about learning to let go of good times, for example a season, a relationship, a holiday, or even life. On your own, or in a small group, discuss what themes you think are important here.

## Activity 5

### Context

John Keats wrote this poem towards the end of his life, and probably knew he did not have long to live when he wrote it, as he had tuberculosis, and died when he was only 25.

How does this biographical knowledge affect your reading of the poem?

Keats was one of the Romantic poets; his poems focus on feelings and celebrate nature. He is well known for writing a series of odes, of which 'To Autumn' was the last.

### Support

Draw illustrations or find photos to represent some of the key **images** in the poem. Make them into a poster, with relevant quotations from the poem to support the images.

### Stretch

Keats was a keen letter-writer. Carry out some research into his letters, and find the letter he wrote about the inspiration behind 'To Autumn'. How might this enhance your understanding of the poem?

# 'Afternoons' by Philip Larkin

## Learning objectives

- To understand the key ideas of the poem, by tracking through its detail
- To form an overview of the poem's content, themes, the way it is written, and its context

### Key terms

**Stanza:** another word for a verse in poetry

**Tone:** the feeling behind what is written. It could be calm, angry, shocked or surprised, for example

**Enjambement:** where the sense of a line carries on from one line to the next, without a pause

**Tip** Writers often use times of the day or seasons of the year to suggest the different stages in life. So afternoon and early autumn would suggest that the best (midday and summer) is past.

### Activity 1

**First impressions**

a. As you read this poem, reading from punctuation mark to punctuation mark, make a note of the different pictures, or ideas, that come to mind.

b. What feelings do you get about the young women and children in the first **stanza**?

c. The second stanza gives some insight into the home lives of the same young mothers. What impressions do you get?

d. What feelings about the lives of the young mothers do you get from the final stanza? Give reasons for what you say.

### Activity 2

**Looking at the detail**

a. What effect is given by the time of year suggested in the poem?

b. What do you think is suggested by 'the hollows of the afternoons'?

c. Look at the pattern of the phrases 'Behind them' and 'Before them' in the second stanza. What might this suggest about the lives of the young women?

d. Why do you think the wedding albums are described as 'lying/Near the television'? There may be more than one interpretation here.

e. Why do you think 'unripe acorns' are mentioned in the final stanza?

f. What does the poet mean by 'Something is pushing them/To the side of their own lives'?

g. What do you think of the **tone** of the speaker in the poem, who seems to be some sort of observer? It may be cynical, melancholic, reflective, matter of fact – or maybe a combination of all these. Find parts of the poem that would support these ideas.

### Activity 3

**Structure**

a. The poem is organized into three regular stanzas. How might this fit into the overall meaning of the poem?

b. What might be the effect of the second stanza using **enjambement** to link to the final stanza?

## Activity

### Themes

Some possible themes here are marriage, relationships, growing up, change, identity. Can you think of any others? Which are the most important themes, and why?

## Activity 5

### Context

Philip Larkin wrote most of his poems in the mid-20th century, and this one was probably written in the late 1950s. It seems to be set around the mid- to late 1950s, in a working-class setting. What clues in the poem suggest this?

#### Support

Write an article for a website on the lives of the young women on the estate featured in the poem. You may include interviews with the women, and, perhaps, other people.

#### Stretch

Imagine you are one of the young women from the poem. Write about your life, in prose or poetry.

# 'Dulce et Decorum Est' by Wilfred Owen

## Learning objectives

- To understand the key ideas of the poem, by tracking through its detail
- To form an overview of the poem's content, themes, the way it is written, and its context

### Activity 1

## First impressions

a. As you read the poem, aloud if possible, work out the story of what's going on. It paints a graphic picture of an incident during the First World War.

b. What impressions do you get of the soldiers in the first **stanza**?

c. Describe in your own words what happens next, starting at the end of the first stanza.

d. What do you find out about the condition of the soldier who has been gassed?

e. What are the poet's (or speaker's) feelings at the end of the poem? It may help you to know that the Latin sentence 'Dulce et decorum est pro patria mori' translates as 'It is sweet and fitting to die for your country.'

### Activity 2

## Looking at the detail

a. This is a very vivid description of what it was like to be on the battlefields of the First World War. Owen's choices of words and phrases help to make it vivid. From the start, which **similes** are used to describe the soldiers? What effect does this have on your impressions of the soldiers?

b. 'Blood-shod' is a very succinct expression. What picture does it create?

c. The soldiers are described as 'lame', 'blind', 'drunk' and 'deaf'. Why do you think Owen chose these words?

d. What is the effect of the direct speech at the beginning of the second stanza?

e. Notice how all the focus is then on the single soldier. How might this be effective?

f. When the words of the poet are then addressed to the reader, what effect does this have?

g. Note how the senses are appealed to, particularly in the final stanza. How is this effective?

h. What about the images in the last two stanzas? What impact do they have on you?

### Activity 3

## Structure

a. Notice how the poem builds up, from the shocking description of the soldiers to the bitter, angry **direct address** to 'My friend' at the end. Can you pinpoint each part where the poem moves up a gear?

b. The poem is written in **blank verse**, but the stanzas and even the lines are broken up and 'choppy.' What effect is achieved by this? Think, in particular, of the impact of the two-line third stanza.

## Activity 4

### Themes

War is the obvious theme here, but the themes of patriotism and suffering are also described. Do you think that Owen was angry at the war, or angry at the sort of people addressed at the end of the poem who urge others to go to war without thinking about what it really involves?

## Activity 5

### Context

Wilfred Owen was an officer in the First World War who became increasingly disturbed at what he saw around him. He wrote this poem in 1917, and died on 4th November 1918, only a week before the Armistice was signed marking peace. The church bells were ringing in Shropshire in celebration of the end of the war when the telegram arrived telling his mother of his death.

Do you think this poem and its message are as relevant now, in the 21st century, as they were when it was first written?

#### Support

Write a report on this incident as if you were a soldier reporting back to his officers.

#### Stretch

Read some more of Wilfred Owen's poems, such as 'Futility', 'The Send Off' or 'Disabled.' How might they add to your understanding and appreciation of 'Dulce et Decorum Est'?

# 'Ozymandias' by Percy Bysshe Shelley

## Learning objectives

- To understand the key ideas of the poem, by tracking through its detail
- To form an overview of the poem's content, themes, the way it is written, and its context

### Key terms

**Synecdoche:** where a part represents the whole (such as 'the hand' for 'the sculptor')

**Sonnet:** a traditional poetic form with 14 lines, often split into two parts: an **octave** (eight lines) and a **sestet** (six lines). It traditionally uses the rhythm of **iambic pentameter** (ten syllables or 'beats' to each line, with the pattern of 'te-dum'), which is the rhythm pattern closest to the rhythm of spoken English, so poets often use it to create a conversational tone

**Octave / octet:** eight lines of poetry

**Sestet:** six lines of poetry

**Image / imagery:** pictures in words. They may include similes or metaphors

 **Activity 1**

### First impressions

Before you start reading, it may help you to know that Ozymandias is another name for Rameses II, one of the Pharaohs of Ancient Egypt.

**a.** There are three 'voices' in this poem. Whose are they, and what contribution does each make?

**b.** What do you find out about the statue that the traveller tells of?

**c.** What impressions do you get of the setting of this poem?

 **Activity 2**

### Looking at the detail

**a.** What impressions do you get of the ruler represented by the statue? Give reasons for what you say.

**b.** What do you make of the inscription written on the pedestal (base) of the statue? Be aware that it could have more than one meaning.

**c.** Shelley uses the words 'The hand' to represent the sculptor. This is an example of **synecdoche**. What might be the effect of saying 'the hand' rather than 'the sculptor'?

**d.** What impressions do you get of the sculptor?

 **Activity 3**

### Structure

**a.** The poem is in the form of a **sonnet**. Does Shelley express different ideas, respectively, in the **octave** and **sestet**? Give reasons for what you say.

**b.** The rhythm and rhyme are very regular here. How does this fit in with the message of the poem?

**Activity 4**

### Themes

This relatively short poem contains a number of themes: power, ambition, the relationship between humans and nature, the transience (or perhaps permanence) of art, pride, dictatorship. With a partner, discuss these possible themes and decide which you think are the most important. Remember that you need to be able to support the points you make.

## Activity 5

### Context

This poem has a particularly interesting background. Shelley, who was one of the most radical Romantic poets, wrote it in 1817 as a sort of competition with his friend, Horace Smith. It was inspired by a huge, partially destroyed statue of Rameses II (Ozymandias) which was being brought from Egypt to the British Museum in London.

It also has a wider relevance. In 2003, for example, when the statue of Saddam Hussein was pulled down in Baghdad, some people saw comparisons with Shelley's sonnet.

Can you think of other situations in the past or present that could also fit in with the poem?

**Tip** Poems can carry their meanings across the years, and even centuries. If a poem chimes in with your own experience, it's fine to say so – even if it was written a long time before you were born.

### Support

Choose one of the key **images** from this poem and illustrate it with an apt quotation. Alternatively, make a poster representing the whole sonnet, with helpful notes for younger students.

### Stretch

Think back to what you have found out about the Romantic poets. What qualities of Romantic poetry are to be found in 'Ozymandias'?

# 'Mametz Wood' by Owen Sheers

## Learning objectives

- To understand the key ideas of the poem, by tracking through its detail
- To form an overview of the poem's content, themes, the way it is written, and its context

### Key terms

**Image / imagery:** pictures in words. They may include similes or metaphors

**Personification:** making something not alive sound as if it is alive

**Stanza:** another word for a verse in poetry

 **Activity 1**

### First impressions

Before you start reading, it may be helpful to know that Mametz Wood was the site of a battle in the First World War, visited by the poet, Owen Sheers, in the 21st century.

As you read the poem, what feelings do you have about what happened there, and what do you find out about what is still happening there now?

Think about what the local farmers are finding as they turn over the land, and what has recently been unearthed, literally.

 **Activity 2**

### Looking at the detail

a. Who do you think are 'the wasted young'? What is the effect of the word 'wasted'?

b. There are a lot of **images** of fragility used to describe the bone fragments that are found. Make a note of these images and explain how they are effective.

c. What impression of the earth is given in the **personification** 'stands sentinel'?

d. What is the effect of the image in the final line of the fourth **stanza**, of 'a wound working a foreign body to the surface of the skin'?

e. What impact does the graphic imagery of the skeletons in the uncovered grave have on you? Give reasons for what you say. It may help if you find some illustrations of a *danse-macabre*.

f. What do you make of the final stanza, with its reference to 'the notes they had sung'?

g. What is the tone of the poem? Is it reflective? Thoughtful? Sad? Angry? Give reasons for what you say.

 **Activity 3**

### Structure

a. How might the poem's structure of three-line stanzas, so that they appear almost as layers, be effective?

b. There are only five sentences in the whole poem. Read the poem divided into sentences as units of sense. What stages does it break up into?

c. Look at the sentence describing the skeletons. It is written so that you have to read it almost without pausing. What impact does this have?

## Activity 4

**Themes**

The most obvious themes here are war, the influence of the past on the present, and the relationships between humans and nature and the land. Which do you think are the most important, and why?

## Activity 5

**Context**

Mametz Wood is in northern France, where, in the First Battle of the Somme in July 1916, the 38th (Welsh) Division were commanded to attack German soldiers concealed in the wood. Although they finally succeeded, it was at the cost of some 4000 killed or injured. Owen Sheers, a Welsh poet, visited the site of this battle almost 100 years later, and this poem describes his experiences and thoughts.

How does this knowledge affect your interpretation of the poem and its themes?

**Support**

Imagine you were interviewing Owen Sheers about his visit to Mametz Wood. What questions would you ask him?

**Stretch**

Carry out some additional research into what happened at Mametz Wood and produce a fact file on it for future English Literature students.

# Excerpt from 'The Prelude' by William Wordsworth

## Learning objectives

- To understand the key ideas of the poem, by tracking through its detail

- To form an overview of the poem's content, themes, the way it is written, and its context

### Key terms

**Image / imagery:** pictures in words. They may include similes or metaphors

**Sibilance:** a sort of hissing sound, created by repeating 's' or 'sh' sounds

**Blank verse:** ten-syllable lines, almost always in iambic pentameters

### Activity 1

#### First impressions

a. Read the excerpt from 'The Prelude' straight through, and try to imagine the scene being described.

b. What time of day is it, and what season of the year? What is the weather like? How do you know?

c. How does the young Wordsworth (the 'I' in the poem) respond to the different experiences described here? What impressions do you get of him?

d. What impressions do you get of the setting?

### Activity 2

#### Looking at the detail

a. Look at all the references to 'we' and 'us.' What does this suggest about Wordsworth?

b. But notice, too, how he says it was a 'happy time... for all of us' but for him 'It was a time of rapture.' What do you think is suggested by this?

c. How many words and **images** connected to movement can you find? What is the effect of these words and images?

d. Read again the part of the poem that begins with 'All shod with steel', and notice all the 'sh' and 's' sounds. How might this use of **sibilance** suggest what is happening in the poem?

e. There are a lot of references to different sounds in this poem. Make a list of them. What sort of mood and atmosphere do they help create?

f. The echoes in the mountains are described as 'an alien sound/Of melancholy.' How might this alter the mood and atmosphere of the poem?

### Activity 3

#### Structure

This is only an extract from the first of 13 books of 'The Prelude'. The whole poem was written in **blank verse**. What effect is achieved by this type of verse? Remember it is the natural rhythm of spoken English.

### Activity 4

#### Themes

What are the main themes here? Childhood? Memories? Nature? The link between humans and nature? Maybe you can think of more, but remember to give reasons for what you say.

## Activity 5

### Context

William Wordsworth was born in Cockermouth, in present-day Cumbria, on the edge of the Lake District, in 1770. His mother died when he was eight, and William and his brothers and sister were split up. William was sent to Hawkshead Grammar School, in the southern Lakes, where he lodged with a woman called Ann Tyson (a common practice in those days). Her cottage may have been one of the lights he could see, and ignored, when he was skating. Wordsworth was an expert ice skater and continued this hobby until he was an old man.

'The Prelude' was, in effect, his autobiography. He worked on it throughout his life and it was his wife who actually gave it its title (and subtitle, 'The Growth of a Poet's Mind') after he died.

Wordsworth was one of the founders of the Romantic poetry movement. In this excerpt from 'The Prelude' you can find many aspects of Romantic poetry, such as the emphasis on how the everyday activities of ordinary people can spark deep emotions, the awe of nature, and the use of relatively simple and straightforward language.

Annotate (make notes on) a copy of the extract from 'The Prelude', highlighting where it is typical of Romantic poetry.

**Tip**

Even when a poem is strongly autobiographical, like 'The Prelude', don't be tempted to write all you know about a poet's life. Keep your focus on the poem, and only mention biographical details if they are relevant.

### Support

Try writing some lines in blank verse (ten-syllable lines) about a day in your life.

### Stretch

You may like to read some more extracts from 'The Prelude' (or, indeed, the whole poem!) Try the boat-stealing episode, or Wordsworth's account of when he went bird-nesting, in Book 1, or the part in Book 11 in which he witnessed the beginnings of the French Revolution as a young man.

# Putting it all together

## Learning objectives

- To understand the key ideas of the poem, by tracking through its detail
- To form an overview of the poem's content, themes, the way it is written, and its context

### Exam link

In the exam, one poem is printed on the paper, so this is an opportunity to look really closely at detail. To help you when you choose your poem for comparison, a list of all the poem titles in the Anthology is also printed on the paper.

Look at part (a) of the sample exam question below. Then look at the notes opposite that a student made on the first stanza of 'To Autumn'.

> **(a)** Read the poem below, 'To Autumn', by John Keats.
>
> In this poem, Keats explores ideas about nature. Write about the ways in which Keats presents nature in this poem.

### Activity 1

Continue annotating (making notes on) the rest of the poem opposite.

### Activity 2

Now look at how the student has used their notes to start writing a response to part (a) of the exam question:

In 'To Autumn', John Keats speaks directly to autumn and describes the different stages of nature in this season.

In the first stanza he describes the early stages of autumn, when fruits are ready to be harvested. He starts by describing it as 'season of mists and mellow fruitfulness', which creates a visual image of misty days in autumn, but also suggests that everything is 'mellow' or laid back. The idea of autumn as a person, plotting, or 'conspiring' with the sun in order to ripen the fruits suggests how different elements of nature work together to produce the harvest. The reference to the bees making the most of the last warm days reinforces this feeling, and the rhyming of 'bees' and 'cease' could suggest bees buzzing, so helps suggest the sounds of nature, too.

Addressing Autumn

Sounds peaceful and chilled

Apples about to fall – everything ripe

Working for bees, too – buzzing sound?

Personifies autumn and the sun, as if they are working together

Heavy with fruit

**To Autumn**

Season of mists and mellow fruitfulness!
Close bosom-friend of the maturing sun;
Conspiring with him how to load and bless
With fruit the vines that round the thatch-eaves run;
To bend with apples the moss'd cottage-trees,
And fill all fruit with ripeness to the core;
To swell the gourd, and plump the hazel shells
With a sweet kernel; to set budding more,
And still more, later flowers for the bees,
Until they think warm days will never cease,
For Summer has o'er-brimm'd their clammy cells.

Who hath not seen thee oft amid thy store?
Sometimes whoever seeks abroad may find
Thee sitting careless on a granary floor,
Thy hair soft-lifted by the winnowing wind;
Or on a half-reap'd furrow sound asleep,
Drows'd with the fume of poppies, while thy hook
Spares the next swath and all its twined flowers;
And sometimes like a gleaner thou dost keep
Steady thy laden head across a brook;
Or by a cyder-press, with patient look,
Thou watchest the last oozings hours by hours.

Where are the songs of Spring? Ay, where are they?
Think not of them, thou hast thy music too,—
While barred clouds bloom the soft-dying day,
And touch the stubble plains with rosy hue;
Then in a wailful choir the small gnats mourn
Among the river sallows, borne aloft
Or sinking as the light wind lives or dies;
And full-grown lambs loud bleat from hilly bourn;
Hedge-crickets sing; and now with treble soft
The red-breast whistles from a garden-croft;
And gathering swallows twitter in the skies.

John Keats

**Activity 3**

Continue writing a response about 'To Autumn', using your notes. Don't forget to:

- refer to key words and phrases from the poem, explaining how they are effective in suggesting nature

- include references to the contexts of the poem. For example, you may have discussed:

  - the traditional harvesting methods mentioned in the poem

  - the acceptance of change, which could link into Keats's acceptance of his sickness and likely early death

  - the aspects of Romantic poetry, such as the use of everyday images relevant to ordinary people

- discuss the way the poem is organized

- show an understanding of how nature is presented in the poem.

Now read part (b) of the sample exam question:

> **(b)** Choose **one** other poem from the Anthology in which the poet also writes about nature. Compare the presentation of nature in your chosen poem to the presentation of nature in 'To Autumn'.
>
> In your answer to part (b) you should compare:
>
> - the content and structure of the poems – what they are about and how they are organized
>
> - how the writers create effects, using appropriate terminology where relevant
>
> - the contexts of the poems, and how these may have influenced the ideas in them.

The student decided to use Seamus Heaney's poem, 'Death of a Naturalist', as their second poem to discuss. Read the notes they made on this poem:

<u>Child's changing views of nature</u>

Starts with description of flax dam:

- 'punishing sun', appeal to senses – bluebottles
- Child (Heaney?) filling jam jars of frogspawn
- Language of small child (Miss Walls, 'daddy frog', 'mammy frog')
- Learning ('you could tell the weather by frogs too')

Second stanza – change:

- Negative imagery – cow dung, 'angry frogs', 'coarse croaking'
- 'Mud grenades' – danger?
- 'great slime kings' – vengeance for theft of frogspawn: 'If I dipped my hand the spawn would clutch it'
- Title – humour? Only makes sense at end

Now read the student's notes comparing the two poems, 'To Autumn' and 'Death of a Naturalist':

Similarities – personal views of nature, respect for nature, set in countryside, appeal to senses. Structure of stanzas suggests changes. Both written in blank verse to give conversational tone. Both use imagery to create impressions of nature.

Differences – Keats – different aspects of specific season; Heaney – focus on frogs, understanding of nature

Titles – 'To Autumn' (straightforward), 'Death of a Naturalist' (not clear at first)

Heaney – seems autobiographical; Keats – more of an observation, poet not so obviously involved?

Settings – rural Ireland (including junior school) for Heaney; flax dams, etc. Very localized. Keats – no specific place, but traditional 19th-century rural scenes (references to harvesting)

## Exam link

In the exam, there are 15 marks for part (a) and 25 marks for part (b).

So it may help to divide the time into roughly:

- 20 minutes on the first poem (including reading and making notes on it)
- 40 minutes on the second poem (including reading and making notes on it, and comparing it with the first poem).

In part (b), you may compare as you go through, or leave the comparison until the end. Whichever approach you choose, make sure you don't skim over the second poem.

## Activity

Try writing your response to part (b) of the exam question, using 'Death of a Naturalist' by Seamus Heaney as your choice of poem to compare with 'To Autumn' by John Keats. You may use the ideas in the notes on page 67, but you may also add some ideas of your own. In your response to part (b) you should also explore similarities and differences between 'Death of a Naturalist' and 'To Autumn'.

## Progress check

Have you:

1. written in as much detail as you can about 'Death of a Naturalist' (without having the text of the poem in front of you)?
2. made clear points about similarities and differences between the two poems?
3. made references to the content, messages, style and contexts of both poems?
4. used words associated with comparing and contrasting to organize your answer?
5. given your personal response to the poems?

## Activity (5)

Choose another poem from the Anthology that deals with nature, and make notes on how you would compare it with either 'To Autumn' or 'Death of a Naturalist'.

## Activity (6)

Organize the poems in the Anthology into themes. You will probably find that most of the poems will fall into a number of themes, some of which are:

- love
- war
- conflict
- power
- nature
- childhood
- memories
- death
- loss
- relationships.

List as many themes as you can find, then see which poems fit into which themes. Now choose one theme, and two poems which fit into it. Make notes comparing these two poems, as you did in Activity 5 above.

### Progress check

By now you should be fully confident in your knowledge and understanding of the poems in the Anthology, and how to show this in the exam. Use the questions below as a guide to check that this is the case.

For each question, answer:
✓   yes (fully confident)
✗   no (not at all confident – quite a lot of work to be done)
?   maybe (a bit more work to be done)

| | Yes ✓ | No ✗ | Maybe ? |
|---|---|---|---|
| I understand what each poem in the Anthology is about. | | | |
| I can explain the theme(s) or message(s) for each poem in the Anthology. | | | |
| I can highlight key words and phrases from each poem and explain how and why they are effective. | | | |
| I can make sensible points about the contexts of the poems. | | | |
| I can find points of similarity and difference between the poems. | | | |
| I can use a range of words and phrases to highlight these similarities and differences. | | | |

# 3 Post-1914 prose/drama

## Assessment Objectives

In this part of the exam, you will be assessed against these Assessment Objectives:

- **AO1** Read, understand and respond to the text, maintaining a critical style, developing a personal response, and using textual references, including quotations, to support and illustrate interpretations

- **AO2** Analyse the language, form and structure used by a writer to create meanings and effects, using relevant subject terminology where appropriate

- **AO4** Use a range of vocabulary and sentence structures for clarity, purpose and effect, with accurate spelling and punctuation

In this section of the book, you will develop the skills you need to write about the post-1914 prose or drama text you have studied. You will have studied one of these texts:

- *Never Let Me Go*, by Kazuo Ishiguro
- *Anita and Me*, by Meera Syal
- *Lord of the Flies*, by William Golding
- *The Woman in Black*, by Susan Hill
- *Oranges Are Not the Only Fruit*, by Jeanette Winterson
- *An Inspector Calls*, by J.B. Priestley
- *The History Boys*, by Alan Bennett
- *Blood Brothers*, by Willy Russell
- *The Curious Incident of the Dog in the Night-Time*, by Simon Stephens
- *A Taste of Honey*, by Shelagh Delaney

You will get plenty of practice in developing the skills necessary to tackle the exam question. You will:

- develop your detailed knowledge of the set text, its characters and themes
- develop your knowledge of the way it is written and organized.

> **Tip**
> A good way to ensure you are addressing AO2 is to focus closely on the detail of the extract.

## In the exam

You will need to show your close-reading skills by referring to details from a printed extract from the prose or drama text you have studied. You will then extend your discussion as you write about the whole text. This is called a 'source-based question'.

In the source-based question, you will look closely at the extract (or 'source') and answer an essay question on the whole novel or play. You will use the extract as well as details and references from across the whole novel or play, to show your knowledge and understanding.

So you need to address both the extract and the whole text in this question. You have about 45 minutes in which to plan and write your answer, so keep an eye on the time and make sure you don't spend too long on the printed extract.

# 1 Getting started

## Learning objective

- To look closely at the opening of the play or novel studied, and to consider how the situation, characters and themes are introduced, and to identify the way it is written

### Key term

**Juxtaposition:** placing two different things together for contrast

## Activity 1

Whatever the text, a writer wants to catch the attention of their reader or audience immediately, and hold their interest, perhaps by hinting at some possible problem or complication. It is also important to give a clear idea of characters and their relationships, and, perhaps, to introduce some of the text's themes.

Look at the first page or so of the post-1914 novel or play you are studying, and annotate it (make notes) as you read. If you are studying one of the following texts, you could extend your extract a bit further.

For example, here is how the annotated opening of *Oranges Are Not the Only Fruit* might look:

*Matter-of-fact, down-to-earth tone*

*Conflict?*

Like most people I lived for a long time with my mother and father. My father liked to watch the wrestling, my mother liked to wrestle; it didn't matter what. She was in the white corner and that was that.

*Strong character*

She hung out the largest sheets on the windiest days. She *wanted* the Mormons to knock on the door. At election time in a Labour mill town she put a picture of the Conservative candidate in the window.

*Humour in juxtaposition of items*

She had never heard of mixed feelings. There were friends and there were enemies.

*Random items – humour again*

Enemies were:　The Devil (in his many forms)
　　　　　　　　Next Door
　　　　　　　　Sex (in its many forms)
　　　　　　　　Slugs

Friends were:　God
　　　　　　　Our dog
　　　　　　　Auntie Madge
　　　　　　　The Novels of Charlotte Brontë
　　　　　　　Slug Pellets

*A wrestling term – li back to first paragra*

*Hint of conflict to come?*

and me, at first, I had been brought in to join her in a tag match against the Rest of the World. She had a mysterious attitude towards the begetting of children; it wasn't that she couldn't do it, more that she didn't want to do it. She was very bitter about the Virgin Mary getting there first. So she did the next best thing and arranged for a foundling. That was me.

*Reference to narrator's adoption*

I cannot recall a time when I did not know that I was special. We had no Wise Men because she didn't believe there were any wise men, but we had sheep. One of my earliest memories is me sitting on a sheep at Easter while she told me the story of the Sacrificial Lamb. We had it on Sundays with potato.

*Hint of the part religion will play in the story*

And here is how the annotated opening of *The Curious Incident of the Dog in the Night-Time* might look:

Part One

*Shock impact – can't be ignored*
→ *A dead dog lies in the middle of the stage. A large garden fork is sticking out of its side.*

**Christopher Boone**, *fifteen years old, stands on one side of it. His forty-two-year-old neighbour* **Mrs Shears** *stands on the other.*

*They stand for a while without saying anything. The rest of the company watch, waiting to see who is going to dare to speak first.*

*Silence creates tension and anticipation*

**Mrs Shears**  What in Christ's name have you done to my dog?

*Dramatic opening line, made more so by blasphemy*

**Christopher** *is frozen to the spot.*

**Mrs Shears**  Oh no. Oh no. Oh no. Oh Christ.

**Christopher's** *teacher, twenty-seven-year-old* **Siobhan** *opens Christopher's book. She reads from it.*

*Link to title of play*
**Siobhan**  It was seven minutes after midnight. The dog was lying on the grass in the middle of the lawn in front of Mrs Shears' house.

**Mrs Shears**  Get away from my dog.

  [...]

**Siobhan**  There was a garden fork sticking out of the dog. The dog was called Wellington. It belonged to Mrs Shears who was our friend. She lived on the opposite side of the road, two houses to the left.

*Precise tone with short, clipped sentences*

**Mrs Shears**  Get away from my dog.

**Christopher** *takes two steps away from the dog.*

*Siobhan voicing Christopher's words*
**Siobhan**  My name is Christopher John Francis Boone. I know all the countries of the world and the capital cities. And every prime number up to 7507.

*Extraordinary skills – autistic?*

**Mrs Shears**  Get away from my dog, for Christ's sake.

**Christopher** *puts his hands over his ears. He closes his eyes. He rolls forward. He presses his forehead on to the grass. He starts groaning.*

*Sudden and dramatic movement and sound would shock audience*

**Tip**  With plays, always pay close attention to the stage directions. They will help you to develop your understanding of characters, their relationships, mood and atmosphere and themes.

**Tip**

As you read further on in your set text, keep referring back to these notes, and see if your initial ideas have been confirmed or changed.

**Activity 2**

Use the annotations you made on the opening to the novel or play you are studying to jot down a few notes about your ideas under the following headings:

- Content/events
- Impressions of characters
- Themes
- Possible conflict/development
- Style

For example, this is how your notes might look for *Oranges Are Not the Only Fruit*:

| Content/events | Introduction – set in working-class town. Narrator (author?) adopted. |
|---|---|
| Impressions of characters | Daughter very observant. Mother very dominant. Father barely mentioned. |
| Themes | Religion? Growing up? |
| Possible conflict/ development | Between mother and daughter? |
| Style | Humorous, matter-of-fact tone. Use of capital letters – for humour? For emphasis? |

And this is how your notes might look for *The Curious Incident of the Dog in the Night-Time*:

| Content/events | Death of dog (as per title) established. |
|---|---|
| Impressions of characters | Christopher: central character, but doesn't speak (voiced by Siobhan). Autistic? Seems disturbed. Mrs Shears: upset (understandably). |
| Themes | Communication? Mystery? |
| Possible conflict/ development | Solving the mystery of the dead dog. Finding out the source of Christopher's distress. |
| Style | All cast on stage; Siobhan speaking for Christopher. |

## Support

Write up your notes on the opening to the set text you are studying, answering the following questions:

**a.** What do you think of the opening of the novel or play you are studying?

**b.** Write about characters and events, and about how the opening catches the interest of the reader or audience.

## Stretch

Using your notes, write in response to the following questions:

**a.** To what extent do you find the opening of the novel or play you are studying effective?

**b.** Include your responses to:

- the introduction of characters
- the setting of the scene
- the way it is written
- the way it may prepare a reader or an audience for how the novel or play may develop.

**What happens**

## Learning objective

- To determine the key events in the plot, or story, of the text studied, and how these may reflect the structure of the text

### Key term

**Chronologically:** arranged in the order in which events actually happened

**Tip** Think of your brief summary as the bones of a skeleton, which you will flesh out by adding detail from the text, as well as through discussion.

Texts, whether plays or novels, will fall naturally into 'chunks' or sections. The story may be told **chronologically**, with one thing happening after another, or through a series of flashbacks, but there will be significant events that shape the action of the story happening throughout the text.

Some stories divide naturally into phases of the characters' lives (*Blood Brothers* and *Never Let Me Go* are good examples of this).

### Activity 1

Working on your own, or in a small group, look back at the novel or play you are studying and see whether it falls into chunks as described above.

Then, make notes of the key events that take place in each chunk.

Finally, choose one event in each chunk that you think is the most important, perhaps in developing the story, or a character, or providing a climax.

You have now created a brief summary of your text, which you can refer to or build on later.

### Activity 2

Present your ideas to the rest of the class, and see how your ideas are similar or different.

#### Support

Give a title, like a sort of heading or headline, to each chunk of text.

#### Stretch

Choose a key quotation (as brief as possible) for each chunk.

### Activity 3

You are going to tackle 'the six-word challenge'. It was supposedly started by the novelist Ernest Hemingway when he was challenged to write a short story in only six words. His read:

> 'For sale:
> baby shoes, never worn.'

Working on your own, or with a partner, see if you can capture the essence of the novel or play you are studying in only six words.

## Support

Carry out some research on the Internet into some six-word stories that have been published in the 21st century.

## Stretch

Try to create a six-word story for some of the characters in the text you are studying.

## Activity 4

Write a 'blurb' (piece of publicity text) for the play or novel you are studying – like that found on the back covers of books or on publishers' websites. The 'blurb' should sum up the main features of the text, such as its broad storyline, themes, and characters, and mention which readers may enjoy it. The key here is to be as succinct as possible – and not to give away too much!

# 3 Looking at characters

## Learning objective

- To look in detail at the presentation of characters and relationships in the novel or play studied

## Activity 1

Whether you are studying a play or a novel, a good way to start discussing a character is to examine the way the reader or audience is introduced to them. This may be through:

- stage directions (in a play)
- what other people say about them
- their first words
- how they are described (in a novel)
- or a combination of the above.

Choose one of the main characters in the text you are studying and find the first references to them, either in stage directions (for a play), their first words or description, or what others say about them.

Make notes on what clues to the character are provided.

For example, here are possible notes on Eric Birling from the play, *An Inspector Calls*:

| First mention | In the stage directions at the beginning of the play, Eric could be interpreted as being slightly separated from the rest of the family. His parents are seated at each end of the dining table, and his sister and her fiancé, Gerald Croft, are sitting together on one side, leaving Eric on his own on the other. |
|---|---|
| Description | Also in the stage directions, Eric is described as 'in his early twenties, not quite at ease, half shy, half assertive.' Interesting – why not at ease? |
| First words | Eric in fact does not speak at all for some time, while the rest of the family are celebrating Sheila and Gerald's engagement. (Significant, perhaps?) The first time he makes a sound is when he bursts out laughing ('suddenly guffaws') and when Sheila asks him what the joke is he seems awkward: 'I don't know – really. Suddenly I felt I just had to laugh'. He is then accused by Sheila of being 'squiffy' (drunk) which he quickly denies, as the two of them bicker. |
| Conclusions | Eric seems not to fit into the happy family picture very well. He seems awkward, with something to hide, and there seems to be tension between him and his sister. |

And here are possible notes on Nanima, the grandmother of the central character, Meena, in the novel *Anita and Me*:

| First mention | When Meena is talking about how her only knowledge of her grandparents was 'in the framed photographs that hung in my parents' bedroom... Mama's mother, my Nanima, looked like a smaller, fatter version of her, all bosom and stomach and yielding eyes.' (Comforting image?) Introduced as the 'help from overseas' promised by the fortune teller at the fair, to help the family when Mama is suffering from post-natal depression. (Almost magical properties?) |
|---|---|
| Description | 'My Nanima's arrival did not go unnoticed in the village.' (Noisy welcome, bringing family together.) 'Papa flung open the Mini door ceremoniously; and Nanima levered herself out, brushing out the creases in her beige salwar kameez suit with gnarled brown fingers and pulling her woollen shawl around her...' |
| First words | (As she hugs Meena) 'Suddenly I was in the middle of a soft warm pillow which smelt of cardamom and sweet sharp sweat, and there was hot breath whispering in my ear, endearments in Punjabi which needed no translation...' |
| Conclusions | Nanima is important to Meena before she even meets her, and the build-up to her arrival confirms this. There is a strong sense of security and reassurance once they finally meet, even though they do not speak the same language. |

## Activity 2

Find the *last* time your chosen character appears, or is mentioned, and see if they have changed, and how.

Then find the key points of their story within the novel or play.

Write up these findings as notes, including a key quotation for each stage of their story.

## Exam link

Remember that in the exam for this question there are up to five marks available for using a range of vocabulary and sentence structures, for clarity, purpose and effect, with accurate spelling and punctuation. So make sure, for a start, that you can spell the names of all the characters in the set text you are studying.

## Activity 3

Conflict between characters is common in plays and novels, whether it is physical conflict, conflicting ideas, or an argument.

Choose a part of the play or novel you are studying where there is conflict and, with a partner, improvise a scene where two characters discuss their differences.

Prepare for it separately, from the point of view of each chosen character. It's a good idea not to rehearse it too much, but to just see what emerges.

You could do your improvisation in front of another pair of students, and afterwards discuss which character you all had the most sympathy for, and why. You may not all agree, but that's fine, as long as you make a good case for your opinions.

### Support

Imagine you are one of the people involved in this conflict. Write down your thoughts and feelings about it.

### Stretch

Imagine that one of the characters involved in the conflict has asked you for advice about the situation you have just improvised. Write down what you would say to them.

## Activity 4

Characters often behave out of character.

Working on your own, with a partner, or in a small group, talk about times when characters in the play or novel you are studying behave differently from how they normally would, and the effect this has on them, and on other characters and/or events in the story.

> **Tip** Think about what makes you sympathize, or not, with characters in the novel or play you have studied. You could also make notes on this, to help with your preparation for the exam.

# 4 Looking beyond the story

## Learning objective

- To explore beneath the surface of the novel or play studied, and discuss its themes

### Key term

**Theme:** the text's 'message'; what the writer wants you to think about

**Themes** are rooted in the storyline of novels or plays, but are broader, so a theme may be common to a range of texts, including poetry, novels and plays, whenever they were written. One way of defining a theme is to think of it as the messages of the text, or what the writer may have wanted you to think about. Most novels and plays will have several themes, with some more obvious than others.

### Activity 1

Working on your own, with a partner, or in a small group, brainstorm (quickly write down, without discussing) all the themes or messages you think are associated with the novel or play you are studying.

Here, for example, is the result of a brainstorm on the themes in the novel *Never Let Me Go*, by Kazuo Ishiguro:

> growing up
>
> love
>
> friendship
>
> death
>
> lies
>
> deceit
>
> identity
>
> hopes and dreams
>
> freedom
>
> memories
>
> the importance of art and creativity
>
> science

And here is the result of a brainstorm on the themes in the play *Blood Brothers*, by Willy Russell:

> money
>
> education
>
> male/female relationships
>
> fate
>
> society
>
> nature v nurture
>
> social class
>
> love
>
> friendship
>
> growing up

If you are studying *Never Let Me Go* or *Blood Brothers*, you may be able to think of other themes, so just add them to the brainstorm.

## Activity 2

**a.** Now that you have gathered together all the themes you can think of for the novel or play you are studying, try to group them in clusters. For example, you may think that friendship, love, and male/female relationships could be grouped together. Some themes may fit into different clusters, and that's fine, too.

**b.** Present these clusters of themes in poster form, and add short, apt quotations to each cluster.

## Activity 3

Working in a small group, decide on a rank order of themes or clusters of themes in your novel or play, working from the one you think is most important to the one you think is least important.

Be prepared to defend your decisions when you share your findings with another group.

## Activity 4

Working either on your own or in a group, prepare a presentation on what makes your novel or play a good one for people of your age to study.

Points to include are:
- its storyline
- its characters
- its themes
- its relevance to people of your age.

**Tip** It's a good idea to think what people may say *against* it being a good text to study, so you can tackle any potential objections head on!

### Support

Write a brief introduction to your novel or play, to be included in a booklet for students who will be studying it in the future. Include enough detail to gain their interest, but not too much, as you don't want to give the story away!

### Stretch

Write up the ideas you gathered for your presentation from Activity 4 as an article for a blog for students of your age.

# 5 Looking at the details

## Learning objectives

● To further develop close-reading skills, using extracts from the novel or play studied

● To understand how writers use language and stylistic features to create a sense of place

### Key terms

**First person:** the speaker's point of view, shown by words like 'I', 'me', 'we', 'us'

**Image / imagery:** pictures in words. They may include similes or metaphors

### Activity 1

**a.** Look at the annotated extract from the novel *The Woman in Black*, by Susan Hill, and, either on your own or with a partner, decide how the writer creates a sense of place.

**b.** What sort of story would you expect this extract to come from?

It was a Monday afternoon in November and already growing dark, not because of the lateness of the hour – it was barely three o'clock – but because of the fog, the thickest of London peasoupers[1], which had hemmed us in on all sides since dawn – if, indeed, there had been a dawn, for the fog had scarcely allowed any daylight to penetrate the foul gloom of the atmosphere.

> *Sense of being trapped; **first person** makes it more immediate.*

Fog was outdoors, hanging over the river, creeping in and out of alleyways and passages, swirling thickly between the bare trees of all the parks and gardens of the city, and indoors, too, seething through cracks and crannies like sour breath, gaining a sly entrance at every opening of a door. It was a yellow fog, a filthy, evil-smelling fog, a fog that choked and blinded, smeared and stained. Groping their way blindly across roads, men and women took their lives in their hands, stumbling along the pavements, they clutched at railings and at one another, for guidance.

> *Sense of fog being inescapable*

> *Unpleasant **imagery***

> *Humans seem lost and vulnerable*

Sounds were deadened, shapes blurred. It was a fog that had come three days before, and did not seem inclined to go away and it had, I suppose, the quality of all such fogs – it was menacing and sinister, disguising the familiar world and confusing the people in it, as they were confused by having their eyes covered and being turned about, in a game of Blind Man's Buff[2].

> *Changed world*

> *Fog almost has a life of its own*

It was, in all, miserable weather and lowering to the spirits in the drearest month of the year.

[1] peasouper: a very dense fog caused by air pollution
[2] Blind Man's Buff: a children's game where one person is blindfolded and, often, spun around, making them disorientated, before trying to catch the other players

Points you may have noticed:

- sense of darkness, being lost, and of being trapped
- unpleasant mood and atmosphere
- appeal to the senses
- features of mystery or ghost stories?

**Exam link**

In the exam, the source-based question will ask you to discuss the novel or play as a whole through a focus such as character, theme or setting. To get you started, the extract printed on the paper will relate to this focus. You should use the extract to demonstrate your close-reading skills (A02), but also to move your discussion on to the whole novel or play, through the focus stated in the question.

### Activity 2

a. Look at the annotated extract from the play *A Taste of Honey*, by Shelagh Delaney, and, either on your own or with a partner, decide how the writer has created a sense of place.

b. What do you learn about the place where the extract is set?

The play is about a pregnant teenager, Jo, whose mother has abandoned her in their flat, while she has gone off with a boyfriend. Geof is her gay friend, who has moved in to help look after her.

| | |
|---|---|
| **Jo** | God! It's hot. |
| **Geof** | I know it's hot. |
| **Jo** | I'm so restless. |
| **Geof** | Oh, stop prowling about. |
| **Jo** | This place stinks. [*Goes over to the door. Children are heard singing in the street.*] That river, it's the colour of lead. Look at that washing, it's dirty, and look at those filthy children. |
| **Geof** | It's not their fault. |
| **Jo** | It's their parents' fault. There's a little boy over there and his hair, honestly, it's walking away. And his ears. Oh! He's a real mess! He never goes to school. He just sits on that front doorstep all day. I think he's a bit deficient. |

[*The children's voices die away. A tugboat hoots.*]

His mother ought not to be allowed.

| | |
|---|---|
| **Geof** | Who? |
| **Jo** | His mother. Think of all the harm she does, having children. |

*Annotations:*
- Humouring her? (→ "I know it's hot.")
- Contrast with negativity? (→ "Oh, stop prowling about.")
- Negative imagery – depressed area
- Zooms in on detail about an individual (→ "There's a little boy over there")
- Docks nearby? (→ "A tugboat hoots")
- Maintaining negative atmosphere (→ "Think of all the harm she does")

Points you may have noticed:

- general sense of poverty and depression
- appeal to the senses – sound effects of children and tugboat, 'stinks', 'colour of lead'
- use of contrast – between Jo and her restlessness, and Geof's calm influence; inside the flat and outside the flat
- the environment seems deprived and poverty stricken, although the sound of children singing introduces a happier note.

## Activity 3

a. Choose an extract from the text you are studying where the writer creates a particular sense of place. The extract you choose should ideally be about half to two thirds of a page long (and no more than a page).

b. Annotate (make notes on) the extract you have chosen, focusing closely on details from the extract.

c. Sum up how the writer has created a sense of place in the extract you have chosen.

### Support

Write an 'extra' scene for the novel or play you are studying, aiming to create a similar sense of place as the one you have just been focusing on.

### Stretch

Find an extract from the novel or play you are studying where the writer creates a different sense of place from the one you have just been focusing on.

What makes it different? Is it:

- what's happening?
- the presence of characters and how they are behaving?
- the imagery used?
- something else?

## Progress check

Look at the table below, which summarizes what you should have learned so far in this section. For each point, give yourself a mark out of 10: 1 means you have no real idea at all, and 10 means you are fully confident. Be honest! Then you will know which parts you need to go back and study a little – or a lot – more.

| Marks out of 10 | What I've learned so far… |
|---|---|
| | I have studied closely the opening of the text I am studying, and understand how the writer has caught the interest of the reader/audience. |
| | I can summarize key events briefly, but also know how to support them with my detailed knowledge of the text. |
| | I know the significance of the first and last appearances of the main characters, as well as the key points of their story. |
| | I understand how characters relate to one another at different points in the text. |
| | I understand what is meant by key themes. |
| | I can explain how a writer creates a sense of place. |

# 6 The source-based question

## Learning objectives

- To learn how to respond to a source-based question, i.e. a question based on an extract from the post-1914 novel or play you have studied
- To learn how to use planning time – reading, thinking, annotating – effectively

### Exam link

Remember, your answer to the source-based question must cover the whole novel or play, as well as detail from the extract.

### Exam link

You should spend no more than 45 minutes on the whole question, including reading, thinking, making notes and writing the response.
So don't spend too long on the extract!

### Activity 1

a. Working on your own, or in a small group, choose a short extract from the post-1914 novel or play you have been studying. If you are studying *The History Boys* or *Lord of the Flies*, choose a different extract from the ones printed here.

b. Compose a question based on the extract and the novel as a whole; there are some examples in this section from *The History Boys* and *Lord of the Flies*. Your question should focus on the presentation of characters, or on the relationships between characters. The extract should probably be no more than about a page of your text in length.

c. Make notes on (annotate) the extract you have chosen. Then jot down some ideas for how you could extend your ideas into the novel as a whole.

Use the following extracts to give you ideas for how to go about this.

The first extract is from *The History Boys* by Alan Bennett. This play is set in a boys' school in the 1980s, where a group of boys is being prepared to apply for entrance to Oxford and Cambridge universities. Irwin is an inexperienced new teacher; Hector, who is mentioned, is the teacher who has been preparing the boys for their university entrance exams up until now.

> **Question: Write about the relationship between Irwin and the boys and how it is presented at different points in the play.**

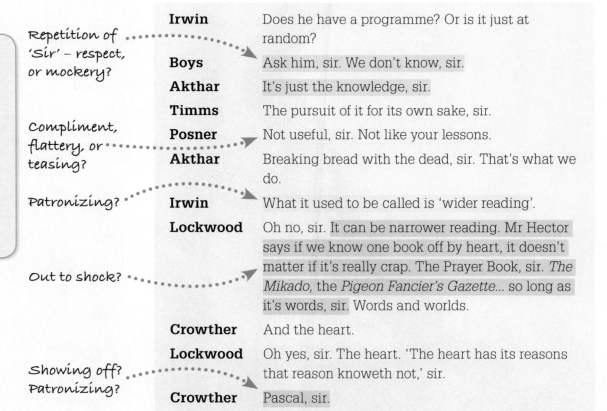

| | |
|---|---|
| **Irwin** | Does he have a programme? Or is it just at random? |
| **Boys** | Ask him, sir. We don't know, sir. |
| **Akthar** | It's just the knowledge, sir. |
| **Timms** | The pursuit of it for its own sake, sir. |
| **Posner** | Not useful, sir. Not like your lessons. |
| **Akthar** | Breaking bread with the dead, sir. That's what we do. |
| **Irwin** | What it used to be called is 'wider reading'. |
| **Lockwood** | Oh no, sir. It can be narrower reading. Mr Hector says if we know one book off by heart, it doesn't matter if it's really crap. The Prayer Book, sir. *The Mikado*, the *Pigeon Fancier's Gazette*... so long as it's words, sir. Words and worlds. |
| **Crowther** | And the heart. |
| **Lockwood** | Oh yes, sir. The heart. 'The heart has its reasons that reason knoweth not,' sir. |
| **Crowther** | Pascal, sir. |

Annotations (handwritten):
- Repetition of 'Sir' – respect, or mockery?
- Compliment, flattery, or teasing?
- Patronizing?
- Out to shock?
- Showing off? Patronizing?

| | |
|---|---|
| **Lockwood** | It's higher than your stuff, sir. Nobler. |
| **Posner** | Only not useful, sir. Mr Hector's not as focused. |
| **Timms** | No, not focused at all, sir. Blurred, sir, more. |
| **Akthar** | You're much more focused, sir. |
| **Crowther** | And we know what we're doing with you, sir. Half the time with him we don't know what we're doing at all. (*Mimes being mystified*.) |
| **Timms** | We're poor little sheep that have lost our way, sir. Where are we? |
| **Akthar** | You're very young, sir. This isn't your gap year, is it, sir? |
| **Irwin** | I wish it was. |

Compliment? But the boys are in control

Highlighting Irwin's youth and inexperience

Seems beaten

**Notes on the whole text**
Irwin's introduction – mistaken by Scripps as 'new boy'
Interview with Headmaster – moustache for classroom control
First meeting with boys – 'brothel scene'
Relationships with boys – their curiosity
Relationship with Dakin
Lessons
Flash forward – meeting with Posner at Rievaulx Abbey
End of play

**Tip** Jot down some notes to help organize the areas you want to cover, but keep these as brief as possible.

Make sure you cover key areas of the text – beginning, middle and end, as well as the extract, in your answer.

**Tip** Try different approaches, and see what works for you – but remember that you need to show your knowledge of the whole text as well as the extract.

Read the following examples of essay openings, and see how the students have used the notes from the extract, as well as the notes on the whole text, in their responses.

**Example 1**

Irwin is the 25-year-old teacher employed by the Headmaster to improve the school's chance of getting its students into Oxbridge. As these boys would be in their late teens, Irwin is not that much older than them, and this is evident in this extract where the boys very much have the upper hand. Indeed, Irwin can hardly get a word in, although he may just be observing the boys' attempts to impress him. At the end of the extract, when Irwin says he wishes it was his gap year, there is a suggestion that he is beginning to feel out of his depth.

The audience is first introduced to Irwin by Scripps, the observer, who mistakes him for a 'new boy' and in his interview with the Headmaster he is advised to grow a moustache for 'classroom control.' His first meeting with the boys is when the Headmaster takes him to Hector's class...

**Example 2**

In this extract we see one of the early lessons between Irwin and the boys. The boys may be showing off to Irwin by referring to what they have learned from Hector. When they refer to the different texts they have supposedly studied, and swear, they may be out to shock him, although maybe they want to impress him. The way they call him 'sir' all the time may show their respect but it may also be a way of teasing him and making him feel insecure. The fact that Akthar makes direct reference to Irwin's youth, and asks if it is his gap year, this could be the boys asserting their authority.

Irwin's youth is established from the start, when Scripps mistakes him for a new boy and the Headmaster seems to be expecting problems when he advises Irwin to grow a moustache for 'classroom control.'

When he first meets the boys, the Headmaster takes him to a class where Hector is teaching them French...

## Comments

These approaches to the question are equally valid. Example 1 starts out with an overview, making it clear who Irwin is, then uses detail from the extract and from the rest of the play to develop the answer. Example 2 starts from the extract, and then moves on to the rest of the play.

The advantage to the approach in Example 1 is that the response starts with a clear overview, summing up the character, and filters in useful detail from the extract and the rest of the play from the start.

The advantage to the approach in Example 2 is that it gives you a clear way in, using the detail from the extract before widening the response to discuss the rest of the play.

> **Tip**
> When the question is specific to one character, you can save time when annotating the extract by focusing on parts of the extract where that character features. However you must also skim read the whole extract, to quickly get the gist of it.

The next extract is from *Lord of the Flies*, a novel set on a deserted island where a plane carrying a group of schoolboys has crashed. The boys are learning to survive on their own. In this extract, three of the main characters, Simon, Jack and Ralph, are exploring the island.

> **Question: Write about the character of Jack and how he is presented throughout the novel.**

They scrambled down a rock slope, dropped among flowers and made their way under the trees. Here they paused and examined the bushes around them curiously.

Simon spoke first.

'Like candles. Candle bushes. Candle buds.'

The bushes were dark evergreen and aromatic and the many buds were waxen green and folded up against the light. Jack slashed at one with his knife and the scent spilled over them.          *Violent action*

'Candle buds.'

'You couldn't light them,' said Ralph. 'They just look like candles.'

'Green candles,' said Jack contemptuously, 'we can't eat them. Come on.'          *Impatient. More practical than the others?*

They were in the beginnings of the thick forest, plonking with weary feet on a track, when they heard the noises – squeakings – and the hard strike of hoofs on a path. As they pushed forward the squeaking increased till it became a frenzy. They found a piglet caught in a curtain of creepers, throwing itself at the elastic traces in all the madness of extreme terror. Its voice was thin, needle-sharp and insistent. The three boys rushed forward and Jack drew his knife again with a flourish. He raised his arm in the air. There came a pause, a hiatus, the pig continued to scream and the creepers to jerk, and the blade continued to flash at the end of a bony arm. The pause was only long enough for them to understand what an enormity the downward stroke would be. Then the piglet tore loose from the creepers and scurried into the undergrowth. They were left looking at each other and the place of terror. Jack's face was white under the freckles. He noticed that he still held the knife aloft and brought his arm down replacing the blade in the sheath. Then they all three laughed ashamedly and began to climb back to the track.          *Dramatic movement*          *Hesitates*          *Scared?*

Makes excuses

'I was choosing a place,' said Jack. 'I was just waiting for a moment to decide where to stab him.'

Trying to regain control

'You should stick a pig,' said Ralph fiercely. 'They always talk about sticking a pig.'

'You cut a pig's throat to let the blood out,' said Jack, 'otherwise you can't eat the meat.'

Still held back by civilized feelings

'Why didn't you – ?'

They knew very well why he hadn't: because of the enormity of the knife descending and cutting into living flesh; because of the unbearable blood.

'I was going to,' said Jack. He was ahead of them and they could not see his face. 'I was choosing a place. Next time – !'

A sign of things to come?

He snatched his knife out of the sheath and slammed it into a tree trunk. Next time there would be no mercy. He looked round fiercely, daring them to contradict. Then they broke out into the sunlight and for a while they were busy finding and devouring food as they moved down the scar towards the platform and the meeting.

## Exam link

Keep your response focused on the question all the time. One way of doing this is by using words from the question throughout your response. For this question, about the presentation of a character, references to 'presentation' should appear in every paragraph.

Remember that your response will also be assessed on AO4: vocabulary, sentence structures, spelling and punctuation. See page 6 for more details.

## Notes on the whole text

First view: arrival on island, appearance (black cloak, red hair), head chorister

Relationships with others: conflict with Ralph, bullying Piggy, developing own tribe

Key moments:
* failure to kill pig (extract)
* kills pig
* face-painting
* death of Simon
* death of Piggy (Roger)
* ending – 'little boy' – seen by naval officer

Points to include: need for power; as psychopathic as he seems?

Presented: through events, description, how others respond to him.

## Activity 2

Look at your notes and ideas for Activity 1, and the question you composed for your chosen extract from the text you are studying. Now write the introductory paragraph.

## Activity 3

Working on your own or with a partner, check that you have:

- focused on the question
- used detail from the extract
- made reference to the rest of the play or novel.

## Activity 4

Plan what you would include in each paragraph for the rest of your answer, using the notes you have already made as a guide.

## Activity 5

Write your concluding paragraph or two to the essay response you have been working on.

Aim to sum up some of your key points and, if possible, hold a good idea back, so that you end on a strong point.

For example, read the following concluding paragraphs of a student's answer to the *Lord of the Flies* question on page 91. Note the points that the annotations make.

> **Tip** Words like 'final', 'finally', 'therefore', 'thus', 'and so' give a clear indication to the person reading your response that you are reaching a (planned) conclusion.

*Clear focus on the ending*

*Pick up on symbolism, if relevant*

*Reference to key events*

*Focus on the question*

*Details to support points made*

*Original point to end on, linking with the extract*

Finally, by the end of the novel the way Golding presents Jack suggests that he and his tribe will succeed in ruling the whole island. The fire, once a symbol of hope, is now used as a focal point for the boys' chants of 'kill the pig' and now, so Sam'n'eric tell Ralph, Jack has sharpened a stick at both ends, presumably with Ralph as the target, just as the pig's head had been mounted on a stick before. As the boys, led by Jack, try to smoke Ralph out of hiding, the fire spreads, and as Ralph flees for his life, pursued by the savage Jack, he ends up at the feet of a naval officer.

The final way Golding presents Jack is through the naval officer's eyes, as opposed to through the eyes of the other boys, and this is a very different Jack. He is described as not a painted monster, but 'a little boy' wearing the remains of a black cap on his red hair and with 'the remains of a pair of spectacles at his waist.' He doesn't even have the nerve to speak to the naval officer, reminding the reader of how he was too scared to kill the piglet earlier.

## Activity 6

Look back at the concluding paragraphs you have written and check that you have done most of the following:

- used words to signal it is the conclusion
- referred to some key events
- referred to the last time we see the character you are writing about/the end of the play or novel
- managed to end on a strong point.

### Support

Write down what you have learned about writing a good source-based essay response.

Include points about:

- planning
- making notes
- focusing on the question
- organizing your answer
- organizing your time.

### Stretch

Choose another extract to use as the basis for a source-based response. This time, choose a different focus: on a theme, setting or creation of a sense of place, for example.

Write your own question to fit the extract you have chosen.

Annotate the extract.

Plan your response, including an introduction and conclusion.

### Progress check

By now you should be fully confident in your knowledge and understanding of the post-1914 play or novel you have studied, and how to show this in the exam. Use the questions below as a guide to check that this is the case.

For each question, answer with:

✓ yes (fully confident)

✗ no (not at all confident – quite a lot of work to be done)

? maybe (a bit more work to be done)

| | Yes ✓ | No ✗ | Maybe ? |
|---|---|---|---|
| I know the story of the text I have studied, and its key events. | | | |
| I know about the characters in the text I have studied, and can discuss their relationships with others. | | | |
| I understand the themes or messages of the text I have studied. | | | |
| I can explain how these themes are shown through events and characters. | | | |
| I can focus on detail in extracts. | | | |
| I can explain how writers create specific effects through their choice of words. | | | |
| I know how to tackle the source-based question. | | | |

# 4 The 19th-century novel

In this section you will develop the skills you need to write about the 19th-century novel you have studied (*Pride and Prejudice* by Jane Austen, *A Christmas Carol* by Charles Dickens, *Jane Eyre* by Charlotte Brontë, *Silas Marner* by George Eliot, *War of the Worlds* by H. G. Wells or *The Strange Case of Dr Jekyll and Mr Hyde* by Robert Louis Stevenson).

You will get plenty of practice in developing the skills necessary to tackle the exam question. You will:

- develop your detailed knowledge of the novel, its characters and themes

- develop your knowledge of how it is written and organized

- acquire an understanding of the relationships between the novel and the context in which it was written.

## Assessment Objectives

In this part of the exam, you will be assessed against these Assessment Objectives:

- **AO1** Read, understand and respond to the text, maintaining a critical style, developing a personal response, and using textual references, including quotations, to support and illustrate interpretations

- **AO2** Analyse the language, form and structure used by a writer to create meanings and effects, using relevant subject terminology where appropriate

- **AO3** Show understanding of the relationships between texts and the contexts in which they were written

## In the exam

You will need to show your close-reading skills by referring to details from a printed extract from the novel you have studied, then extending your discussion as you write about the whole novel. This is called a 'source-based question'.

In it, you will look closely at the extract (or 'source') and answer an essay question on the whole novel. You will use the extract, as well as details and references from the whole novel, to show your knowledge and understanding.

You will also be assessed on your understanding of the context of the novel. This may mean the time and place where it is set or was written, and also the social structures in it (such as families, types of characters, businesses) and the type of novel it is (for example, the Gothic novel). The context may also include the author's background, or how different audiences might respond to the text, if that is relevant to the novel. In all cases, what you write must link to the novel, its characters and events.

# Background to the 19th century

The 19th century was a time of huge change. (If you think back to everything that has happened in the last hundred years, you will realize how much can change in that time frame.)

Listed below, in no particular order, are some key features of the 19th century. As you read this list, think about the impact these developments may have had on the novel you have studied.

## Some key inventions:

- The word 'scientist' was used for the first time (in 1833).

- Lightbulbs, the telephone, the typewriter, the sewing machine, postage stamps, photography, bicycles, film, motorcars, zips, the railway and steam trains, and anaesthesia for tooth extractions were all invented.

## Significant developments:

- Limitation of child labour

- Abolition of slavery

- Growth of the British Empire, after the defeat of France at the beginning of the century

- Introduction of compulsory education

- Serialization of novels in magazines

- General development of scientific knowledge

- Growing debate about status of women

- Beginning of change to the social class structure

- Interest in the supernatural

- Popularity of Gothic stories – including elements such as dark, threatening scenery, a sense of mystery and the supernatural, romance, and often involving a large, old house concealing secrets

- Influence of travel abroad

- Development of industry, with more people living in cities and fewer in the country, so less influence of the rural economy (farms, etc.)

- Rapidly growing population, particularly in cities

## Activity

Choose two or three of the developments or features associated with the 19th century and make some notes on how they might apply to the 19th-century text you have studied.

## Some typical qualities of 19th-century novels:

- Thickly plotted, with a lot happening

- A lot of descriptive detail

- A lot of characters

# 1 What's it all about?

## Learning objectives

- To understand the key parts of the 19th-century novel you have studied, and to form an overview of it
- To begin to understand its context, and how that may impact on modern readers

**Tip** A shorter novel will require fewer episodes, but between three and six should be appropriate for all the texts on the set text list.

## Activity 1

Imagine that you are representing a production company proposing to make a TV series based on the 19th-century novel you are studying.

Working individually, or in a small group, create a proposal for the series, summing up:

- its main storyline
- its appeal to a modern audience.

Each proposer should be prepared to answer questions on their suggestions.

Here is an example of a possible proposal for a TV series based on *Silas Marner*, by George Eliot.

*Silas Marner* – the story of how selfless love is the greatest love of all.

Storyline: Silas Marner, who has become a reclusive miser after being betrayed by all that was important to him, is healed by the love of an abandoned child.

Appeal to modern audience: With its themes of betrayal between brothers, lovers and friends, and the redeeming nature of simple country life, together with the trust of children, this is a timeless tale of loyalty and devotion, while also providing an insight into 19th-century society.

## Activity 2

Assume that your initial proposal has been accepted. Now you (and your group, if appropriate) need to create a detailed explanation of how the novel will be broken down into episodes (no more than six, to cover the whole story).

Each episode should have a title that captures the essence of what happens in this part of the novel. The episodes will probably not be evenly divided chapters, so you need to think of the key stages of the novel you have studied.

You cannot include every little detail, so selection is really important – think particularly about how each episode should start and end.

Below is an example from *Silas Marner*.

### *Silas Marner:* episode breakdown

**Episode 1: 'Dark Times in Lantern Yard'**

This episode introduces the main character of Silas Marner, an earnest young man and a member of an inward-looking sect called The Lantern Yard. He suffers from cataleptic fits (a type of seizure where he loses consciousness without falling down). He is betrayed by his best friend, William Dane, who steals the church's money while Marner is sitting with the sick Deacon. Dane frames Marner for the crime, and then steals Marner's fiancée, Sarah.

Marner is found guilty through the drawing of lots, although he believed that God would clear him. Having lost faith in both God and humans, Marner leaves everything he has known.

**Episode 2: 'Isolation in Raveloe'**

Silas Marner walks a long way, and ends up in Raveloe, a village in the country, a very different place from the dark town he has left. He sets up home and business as a linen weaver, on the edge of the village, by some gravel pits. At first he tries to help locals with his knowledge of herbs for medicinal purposes, but, that, together with his fits and short-sightedness, earns him a bad reputation, and he is avoided by all but a kindly local woman called Dolly Winthrop. Silas grows increasingly isolated, and the whole meaning of his life becomes the gold with which he is paid for his fine linen. He becomes obsessed with counting it, and, and as the years pass, it replaces friends and family in his life.

### Episode 3: 'Gold lost – and found'

In the meantime, there is trouble in the local Squire's household, where Squire Cass's son and heir, Godfrey, is being blackmailed by his evil, gambling brother, Dunstan (or Dunsey). Godfrey has a secret wife (an opium addict called Molly Farren) and a baby daughter. There are money problems and, when more debts are called in, Dunstan takes his brother's horse, Wildfire, to sell. He takes the horse on the local hunt and breaks its neck over a jump. On the way home, Dunstan stumbles across Marner's cottage. Seeing a light, he remembers the story of his gold, and, finding the door open (Marner is out on his rounds), steals his gold. Stumbling in the dark, he falls into the water-filled gravel pit, with the money, and is heard of no more – for now.

Marner is distraught at the loss of his gold but the community rally round to help him look for it. Things are starting to change, and on New Year's Eve, as the rest of the community are at a party in the Red House, the drugged Molly Farren is making her way with her daughter to expose Godfrey's secret to his father. She collapses in the snow and dies, and the toddler, seeing Marner's light, goes in, past Marner, standing in a cataleptic state by the door. When he comes round, seeing the baby's golden curls shining in the firelight, he thinks it is his gold returned, but, unlike the cold, hard, gold, the baby's hair is soft and yielding.

### Episode 4: 'Family Lives'

When Marner turns up at the ball in the Red House, Godfrey's main feeling is relief that his secret marriage will not be uncovered, and he encourages Marner to look after the baby. Godfrey can now propose to the real love of his life, Nancy Lammeter, and all seems solved. Times passes and Silas, helped by Dolly Winthrop, in particular, brings up Eppie, as he calls the baby, and a firm bond is made. Godfrey and Nancy marry, and Godfrey eventually becomes Squire. They are unable to have children, and Nancy refuses to adopt, as she feels they are not meant to have children. Godfrey has to keep his daughter a secret.

**Episode 5: 'The Truth Emerges'**

Time has passed, and the gravel pit is being drained. It uncovers the skeleton of Dunstan, and Marner's gold, which he now realizes no longer has any hold over him. Godfrey realizes that it is time for him to confess, and tells all to Nancy, who wishes he had told her much earlier. They visit Marner and Eppie, who is now fond of Dolly Winthrop's son, Aaron. Marner gives Eppie free choice, whether to move to the Red House, or stay with him. She unhesitatingly decides to stay, and Godfrey and Nancy return alone, destined to remain childless forever, but determined to do what they can, in secret, for Eppie.

**Episode 6: 'Happy Ever After?'**

Before Eppie and Aaron marry, she and Silas go back to the Lantern Yard Church, as Marner still hopes to clear his name, but when they get there, everything has gone, and a grim factory is in its place. They return to Raveloe, where Aaron and Eppie marry, in a wedding secretly paid for by Godfrey and Nancy, and intend to live the rest of Marner's life with him in his cottage, recently extended, again with Godfrey's help.

## Activity 3

**a.** Write a script for part, or the whole, of one of the episodes, making sure that the key points of the story are retained.

**b.** What did you find challenging about this?

**c.** Did you manage to maintain the key parts of the story and suggest relationships between characters?

**d.** What does the novel have that cannot be captured in a play/dramatization?

### Support

- In a group, act out key moments from some of the episodes or draw a simple series of freeze-frames to represent them, to present to the rest of the class. They should be able to identify what is happening, as well as the main characters.

- Once the rest of the class has identified the moment and characters represented in the freeze-frame, a key quotation could be chosen to go with it.

- How did this help you with your understanding of the novel?

- What, if anything, did you find difficult or challenging?

# 2 Focus on characters

## Learning objective

- To focus on the characters, both major and minor, thinking about how and why they behave as they do, their relationships with other characters, and how they contribute to the whole novel

**Tip** This timeline should have a broad-brush approach, covering the main points without going into detail.

Create a timeline of important events for one of the main characters in the novel you have studied. Start with a brief explanation of who they are.

This is how the timeline may appear for Elizabeth Bennet, from *Pride and Prejudice* by Jane Austen.

**Name and details:** Elizabeth Bennet (called Lizzie by those closest to her), 20 years old, the second of five daughters of Mr and Mrs Bennet of Longbourn.

Meets Darcy at a ball at Netherfield. Pretty instant dislike! Older sister Jane, however, gets on well with Darcy's friend, Bingley.

Goes to help Jane, who has fallen ill on visit to Netherfield. Mr Darcy more interested, but Elizabeth not.

Meets Wickham, who tells what turn out to be lies about Darcy.

Turns down a proposal from Mr Darcy.

Turns down a proposal from Mr Collins.

Learns truth about Wickham, in a letter from Darcy.

Goes on a trip with her aunt and uncle, the Gardiners. As tourists, they visit Pemberley, Darcy's home, and bump into him. Elizabeth's opinion of him starts to change...

Younger sister Lydia elopes with Wickham.

Elizabeth finds out that Darcy was instrumental in sorting out the potential scandal about Lydia.

Elizabeth and Darcy get engaged, as have Jane and Bingley.

## Support

Make a poster for your chosen character, showing their relationships with other people. Write their name in the middle, then around this write the characters they have, or have had, relationships with. Place the names of those they are closest to nearer to their name, and the names of those they are least close to further away. You may find it helpful to make more than one poster, if a character's relationships with others change significantly between the beginning and the end of the novel.

## Stretch

Find a key quotation to link to each point of the timeline you have created for your chosen character.

## Activity 2

Research the context of the character you are working on, considering the impact of the time in which they lived, and how modern readers may relate to them. How do their behaviour and attitudes reflect society at that time? For example:

*Some points about context in the presentation of Elizabeth Bennet*

*Pride and Prejudice, published in 1813, was one of the first novels to deal with relatively ordinary people. Although they are members of the gentry (below the aristocracy, but above the working and middle class), the Bennets are at the lower end of this class. Like young men and women all over the world, now, just as then, Elizabeth had concerns everyone can relate to: embarrassing parents, close relationships with friends and siblings, troublesome siblings, and meeting The One.*

*However, there were added complications for young women in the 19th century, because marriage was essential if they were to survive. They were not allowed to inherit any wealth from their father, they could not have an independent career, and if things didn't work out, they could not divorce without an Act of Parliament!*

*It must have taken great strength of character for Elizabeth to turn down several proposals of marriage until she was absolutely sure.*

### Exam link

In the exam you should show your understanding of the novel's context, which is also relevant when you are writing about characters.

## Activity 3

a.  Go back to your timeline and select parts of the novel where the character you have been writing about contributes to the themes (main ideas or messages) of the novel. For example, Elizabeth Bennet's character highlights the themes of love, friendship, marriage, social class, and, of course, pride and prejudice.

b.  Draw a spider-diagram with the character's name in the middle, and links to the themes they are associated with.

c.  Try to find a brief but suitable quotation for each theme you have chosen, and add these to the diagram.

d.  You may find it helpful to illustrate each theme with a picture.

## Activity 4

List the minor characters in the novel you have studied, and for each one, jot down what they add to the novel. They may, for example:

*   bring out different aspects of other characters
*   help the development of the story
*   show something of the novel's context
*   add to its themes.

### Exam link

Including knowledgeable references to minor characters can help develop your essay responses.

# (3) The importance of place

## Learning objective

● To focus on the places featured in 19th-century novels, and appreciate how writers use place to structure their texts

With no mass media, and travel being slow and complicated, 19th-century readers would not necessarily have been aware of a range of different locations, so authors needed to go into more detail to paint word pictures of their stories' locations. Some authors would refer to real-life locations, while others would make them up. Real-life locations give a sense of reality to the texts, while fictitious (made-up) locations enable writers to use elements of different places they know, or, sometimes, to use names to suggest something of the atmosphere of the places.

The table below is a 'map' of the places featured in *Jane Eyre*, with a brief outline of the key events that take place in each.

| Place | Characters and key events | Significance |
|---|---|---|
| **1** Gateshead Hall | Orphaned Jane lives here with the Reed family – her aunt and cousins, where she has a miserable life. After a frightening experience when she is locked in the 'red-room', she is sent away. | Symbolism in the name: 'Gate' suggests an opening, as in the opening to her life, while 'head' may suggest the start of her problems. |
| **2** Lowood | Boarding school for orphans, run by the brutal and hypocritical Mr Brocklehurst. Although much of her time at the school is miserable, Jane finds kindness here, from fellow pupil Helen Burns and teacher Miss Temple. Helen dies from consumption. | Symbolism in the name Lowood: still low times for Jane Eyre. Despite the loss of Helen and the harshness of Mr Brocklehurst, Jane learns, from Helen and Miss Temple, lessons of survival and ends up as a teacher in the school. |
| **3** Thornfield | Jane gets a post here as governess to Adèle Varens, a French child, the ward (or daughter?) of the owner, Mr Rochester, who is rarely there. The house is run by a housekeeper, Mrs Fairfax. There is also a mysterious attic on the top floor, with a locked room (and strange noises) and a servant, Grace Poole.<br>When Mr Rochester arrives with some friends, including Blanche Ingram, it seems that there may be an attraction between him and Jane. Another visitor, Richard Mason, is connected with the mystery of the attic, and is attacked there. | Jane's journey to confidence and independence continues. The name 'Thornfield' suggests suffering and, perhaps, constraint. |
| **4** Gateshead Hall | Jane returns to her aunt's house, as her aunt is sick. | A role reversal – Aunt Reed needs Jane and Jane does not refuse her, despite her harsh childhood. |
| **5** Thornfield | Rochester proposes, but at the altar it is revealed that he is already secretly married, to Bertha Mason, the person in the secret room. Jane refuses to run away to France with Rochester as he asks, and, to avoid temptation, leaves hurriedly. | Jane's suffering seems fated to continue. |
| **6** The moors, and Moor House | After wandering, distressed, on the moors, Jane is saved by the Rivers family, who take her in (and turn out to be her cousins).<br>St John Rivers proposes to Jane, inviting her to accompany him to India as a missionary, but she refuses, as she does not love him. | The moors may represent how Jane is lost. |
| **7** Ferndean | On her return to Thornfield, Jane discovers that the house has been burnt to the ground, Bertha is dead, and Rochester is blinded. Jane and Rochester marry. | The name Ferndean suggests greenness and fertility, suitable for a new start (and Jane and Rochester, who regains his sight, go on to have a son). |

## Activity 1

Working on your own, or in a small group, make a 'map' of important locations in your 19th-century text, like the one on page 104. For each location, say something about its significance and what happens there.

### Support

Choose a symbol for each location to represent its importance in the text. You could add the symbols as a 'key' below the map you created in Activity 1.

### Stretch

Choose some key quotations for each location, explaining how they add to the reader's understanding of the text. For example, they may:
- add to the development of a character or relationship
- refer to a theme
- help to create mood and atmosphere.

## Activity 2

Look back at your 'map' of locations, and discuss what each place may show about the contexts of the novel you are studying. For example:

### Exam link

Remember that in the exam, discussion of the novel's contexts should be embedded *throughout* your response, as you discuss the events, characters and themes of the novel you are studying.

Jane's position as a governess at Thornfield is a reflection of what often happened to women like her, with no other means of support, in the 19th century. The confinement to the attic of Bertha, Mr Rochester's mentally-ill wife, may appear shocking today, but at the time, understanding of mental illness was limited. Similarly, Mr Rochester's attitude to women may seem careless and unthinking, adding to the suffering associated with this location (the 'thorns' of Thornfield?). It is only when he suffers himself, by being blinded in the fire, and the rather gothic house is destroyed, that Jane's 'happy ending' can be secured.

# 4 Close focus on detail

## Learning objectives

- To develop close-reading skills
- To practise annotating extracts from the text

Whether you are analysing an extract from 19th-century prose as part of an exam question, or reading parts of the novel or text in close detail in order to support your discussion of characters or themes, getting close to the writer's language is the key to showing your deep understanding of the text you have studied.

Here, you will learn to develop these close-reading skills, by annotating extracts from the text.

Look at how this extract from *The Strange Case of Dr Jekyll and Mr Hyde* has been annotated, highlighting language and its effects. Focus particularly on how the writer has created a sense of place.

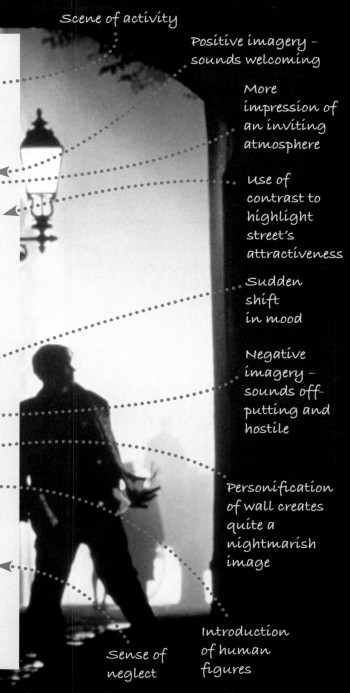

Scene of activity

Positive imagery – sounds welcoming

More impression of an inviting atmosphere

Use of contrast to highlight street's attractiveness

Sudden shift in mood

Negative imagery – sounds off-putting and hostile

Personification of wall creates quite a nightmarish image

Introduction of human figures

Sense of neglect

...their way led them down a by-street in a busy quarter in London. The street was small and what is called quiet, but it drove a thriving trade on the week-days. The inhabitants were all doing well, it seemed, and all emulously[1] hoping to do better still, and laying out the surplus of their gains in coquetry[2]; so that the shop fronts stood along that thoroughfare with an air of invitation, like rows of smiling saleswomen. Even on Sunday, when it veiled its more florid[3] charms and lay comparatively empty of passage, the street shone out in contrast to its dingy neighbourhood, like a fire in a forest; and with its freshly painted shutters, well-polished brasses, and general cleanliness and gaiety of note, instantly caught and pleased the eye of the passenger.

Two doors from one corner, on the left hand going east, the line was broken by the entry of a court, and just at that point, a certain sinister block of building thrust forward its gable on the street. It was two storeys high; showed no window, nothing but a door on the lower storey and a blind forehead of discoloured wall on the upper; and bore in every feature the marks of prolonged and sordid negligence. The door, which was equipped with neither bell nor knocker, was blistered and distained[4]. Tramps slouched into the recess and struck matches on the panels; children kept shop upon the steps; the schoolboy had tried his knife on the mouldings; and for close on a generation no one had appeared to drive away these random visitors or to repair their ravages.

[1] emulously: wanting to do as well, or better
[2] coquetry: flirtatiously – trying to gain attention
[3] florid: bright and obvious
[4] distained: stained, discoloured

Look at another extract, this time from *A Christmas Carol* by Charles Dickens. Examine the way it has been annotated to highlight how the description of a character tells you about the person described, in order to create an overview of your impression of him or her.

*Listing of adjectives emphasizes his negative features*

*Immediate impression of meanness*

*Suggests hardness*

*highlights isolation*

*Words suggesting 'frozen'*

*Suggestion of hidden goodness? Like pearl?*

*Extreme cold*

Oh! But he was a tight-fisted hand at the grindstone, Scrooge! A squeezing, wrenching, grasping, scraping, clutching, covetous old sinner! Hard and sharp as flint, from which no steel had ever struck out generous fire; secret, and self-contained, and solitary as an oyster. The cold within him froze his old features, nipped his pointed nose, shrivelled his cheek, stiffened his gait; made his eyes red, his thin lips blue; and spoke out shrewdly in his grating voice. A frosty rime was on his head, and on his eyebrows, and his wiry chin. He carried his own low temperature always about with him; he iced his office in the dog-days[1]; and didn't thaw it one degree at Christmas.

*Seems entirely self-contained*

External heat and cold had little influence on Scrooge. No warmth could warm, nor wintry weather chill him. No wind that blew was bitterer than he, no falling snow was more intent upon its purpose, no pelting rain less open to entreaty. Foul weather didn't know where to have him. The heaviest rain, and snow, and hail, and sleet, could boast of the advantage over him in only one respect. They often 'came down' handsomely, and Scrooge never did.

*More negative imagery*

*repetition of negatives highlights sense of isolation*

Nobody ever stopped him in the street to say, with gladsome looks, 'My dear Scrooge, how are you? When will you come to see me?' No beggars implored him to bestow a trifle, no children asked him what it was o'clock, no man or woman ever once in all his life inquired the way to such and such a place, of Scrooge. Even the blind men's dogs appeared to know him; and when they saw him coming on, would tug their owners into doorways and up courts; and then would wag their tails as though they said, 'No eye at all is better than an evil eye, dark master!'

*emphasizes how nothing wants to be near him*

But what did Scrooge care? It was the very thing he liked. To edge his way along the crowded paths of life, warning all human sympathy to keep its distance, was what the knowing ones call 'nuts' to Scrooge[2].

*Sums up prior impressions – wholly isolated and hostile character*

[1] dog-days: the hottest days of summer
[2] 'nuts' to Scrooge: pleasurable to him/fine by him

## Activity 1

a. Working on your own, or in a small group, sum up the overall mood and atmosphere of the scene described on page 106. Is it cheerful? Mysterious? Gloomy? Contradictory? Menacing?

b. It may be a mixture of all the above – track through the extract, noting where and how the mood and atmosphere change.

c. Think about the way the writer, Robert Louis Stevenson, has used contrast in order to make an impact and emphasize the different aspects of the scene. Look closely at the way Stevenson's choices of images and words help to create the changing scene.

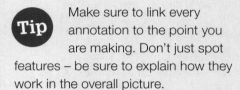

**Tip** Make sure to link every annotation to the point you are making. Don't just spot features – be sure to explain how they work in the overall picture.

## Activity 2

a. Choose an extract from the 19th-century novel you have studied (if it's *The Strange Case of Dr Jekyll and Mr Hyde*, choose another part of the text) where the writer has created a specific sense of place.

b. Annotate (make notes on) the extract you have chosen, and then write a few paragraphs showing how the writer has created the sense of place.

c. How does the sense of place created in the extract you have chosen contribute to the novel as a whole? Does it develop the story, highlight its themes, or add to your understanding of its characters, for example?

### Support

Imagine that the extract you have chosen was illustrated. What sort of colours would be used? And if it was featured in a film, what sort of music would be suitable to play in the background?

### Stretch

Is it possible to sum up the overall mood of the setting in the extract you have been working on, in a single sentence?

## Activity ③

**a.** Working on your own, or in a small group, discuss the impressions of the character (Ebenezer Scrooge) conveyed in the extract on page 107.

**b.** Look at the words and images used and how they are effective in creating your impressions of his character.

## Activity ④

**a.** Choose another extract from the 19th-century novel you have studied where the writer has created a strong sense of character.

**b.** Annotate (make notes on) the extract you have chosen, and then write a few paragraphs showing how the writer has presented the character.

### Exam link

The printed extract in the exam may lead into an essay about the presentation of a character/s, so close focus on the details that relate to character will get you off to a good start.

### Progress check

| In Activity 2 … | Yes | No | Sometimes |
|---|---|---|---|
| … were you specific about the sense of place every time you noted it? | | | |
| … did you choose short quotations to support the points you made? | | | |
| … did you note changes (even small ones) in the scene? | | | |
| **In Activity 4 …** | **Yes** | **No** | **Sometimes** |
| … were you specific in the points you made about your chosen character? | | | |
| … did you look closely at the effects of the words and phrases you selected? | | | |

# 5 The source-based question

## Learning objectives

- To learn how to respond to a source-based question, i.e. a question based on an extract from the 19th-century novel you have studied

- To learn how to use planning time (reading, thinking, annotating) effectively

- To learn how to integrate discussion of context with close reference to the extract and the rest of the text

**Tip** It's important to balance your time when answering this sort of question. It's up to you where you use detail from the extract, but be sure to use detail from across the novel (beginning, middle and end) as well as detail from the extract, in your answer.

**Activity 1**

a. Working on your own, or in a small group, choose a short extract from the 19th-century novel you have been studying, and invent a question based on the extract and the novel as a whole, such as the one below on *A Christmas Carol*. Your question could be based on the presentation of a character, the relationship between characters, or a theme, for example. The extract should probably be about one half to two thirds of a page of your text.

b. Make notes on (annotate) the extract you have chosen. Then make some notes extending your ideas into the novel as a whole. Use the example from *A Christmas Carol* on page 111 to give you ideas on how to go about this.

> **Question: Write about how Dickens presents family life throughout the novel. In your response you should:**
>
> - **refer to the extract and the novel as a whole**
> - **show your understanding of characters and events in the novel**
> - **refer to the context of the novel.**

'Hand-me-downs' – humour

Poor, but making the most of what they can

Then up rose Mrs Cratchit, Cratchit's wife, dressed out but poorly in a twice-turned[1] gown, but brave[2] in ribbons, which are cheap and make a goodly show for sixpence; and she laid the cloth, assisted by Belinda Cratchit, second of her daughters, also brave in ribbons; while Master Peter Cratchit plunged a fork into the saucepan of potatoes, and getting the corners of his monstrous shirt collar (Bob's private property, conferred upon[3] his son and heir in honour of the day) into his mouth, rejoiced to find himself so gallantly attired[4], and yearned[5] to show his linen in the fashionable Parks. And now two smaller Cratchits, boy and girl, came tearing in, screaming that outside the baker's they had smelt the goose, and known it for their own; and basking in luxurious thoughts of sage and onion, these young Cratchits danced about the table, and exalted[6] Master Peter Cratchit to the skies, while he (not proud, although his collars nearly choked him) blew the fire, until the slow potatoes bubbling up, knocked loudly at the saucepan-lid to be let out and peeled.

Happy family scene – large family

'What has ever got your precious father then?' said Mrs Cratchit. 'And your brother, Tiny Tim; And Martha warn't as late last Christmas Day by half-an-hour.'

'Here's Martha, mother,' said a girl, appearing as she spoke.

'Here's Martha, mother!' cried the two young Cratchits. 'Hurrah! There's such a goose, Martha!'

Having to work late on Christmas Eve

'Why, bless your heart alive, my dear, how late you are!' said Mrs Cratchit, kissing her a dozen times, and taking off her shawl and bonnet for her with officious zeal[7].

'We'd a deal of work to finish up last night,' replied the girl, 'and had to clear away this morning, mother.'

Caring mother

Making every effort to look smart for Christmas

'Well. Never mind so long as you are come,' said Mrs Cratchit. 'Sit ye down before the fire, my dear, and have a warm, Lord bless ye.'

'No, no. There's father coming,' cried the two young Cratchits, who were everywhere at once. 'Hide, Martha, hide!'

So Martha hid herself, and in came little Bob, the father, with at least three feet of comforter[8] exclusive of the fringe, hanging down before him; and his threadbare clothes darned up and brushed, to look seasonable; and Tiny Tim upon his shoulder. Alas for Tiny Tim, he bore a little crutch, and had his limbs supported by an iron frame.

Compare with Scrooge not allowing Bob to keep warm by fire

Disabled, but supported (literally) by his father

[1] twice-turned: a thrifty habit, whereby a worn garment was taken apart and sewn back together, inside out, to cover the worn parts
[2] brave: decorated to look pretty
[3] conferred upon: given to
[4] attired: dressed up
[5] yearned: longed
[6] exalted: praised
[7] officious zeal: bossy enthusiasm
[8] comforter: scarf

Notes on the whole text: families
• Scrooge and sister
• Scrooge and Fred
• The 'family' at Fezziwigs
• Belle's family
• The families shown by Ghost of Christmas Present
• Families released from debt by Scrooge's death

## Activity 2

Write the first couple of paragraphs for the response to the question you have just set yourself.

Compare these two openings written by students to the question on *A Christmas Carol* on page 110. Which do you think makes the better start? Why?

**Example 1**

Charles Dickens was born on 7th February 1812 in Portsmouth. He left school when he was a child because his father had been sent to a debtors' prison, and had to go to work in a factory. This must have affected him a lot, and because he was so poor as a child he was determined to be a success. He wrote 'A Christmas Carol' in 1843 and it has been popular ever since.

In this extract, we see the Cratchit family. Bob Cratchit is the clerk of Ebenezer Scrooge and because Scrooge doesn't pay him very much the family live in poverty but are still happy. In Victorian times Christmas was becoming very popular, partly as a result of the influence of Prince Albert, the German husband of Queen Victoria. Christmas is a time for families and this is one of the main ideas in 'A Christmas Carol'. In this extract we see the Cratchit family preparing for Christmas. We see there are a lot of children in the family. This was typical in Victorian times, partly because there was no real birth control and partly because families had lots of children so they could go out to work to help support the family...

**Example 2**

In 'A Christmas Carol', families and family life are presented in a way that makes the reader reflect on their life and relationships, and the novel underlines and emphasizes the importance of the love that is shared within a family. This is evident in this extract where The Ghost of Christmas Present takes Scrooge to witness the preparations for Christmas in the 'four-roomed house' of his clerk, Bob Cratchit, and shows him that although they are clearly suffering from great poverty, as evidenced in their clothes, such as Peter wearing his father's shirt, and Bob's 'threadbare clothes darned up and brushed, to look seasonable', they nevertheless celebrate this special day. Mrs Cratchit, for example, has decorated her 'twice-turned gown' with ribbons, 'which are cheap.'

Not only this, but we see that Martha has to go out to work long hours, in order to supplement the family's income, while the youngest, Tiny Tim, is crippled. Poor Victorian families had to be self sufficient and support themselves, unless there turned out to be a benefactor, such as Scrooge at the end of the novel. Charles Dickens, through the Ghost of Christmas Present, uses the Cratchit family, particularly Tiny Tim's plight, as a key influence to turn Scrooge's life around. Indeed, all three ghosts that visited Scrooge on Christmas Eve showed him one family or another...

If you've chosen Example 2, that's the right answer!

Although there is nothing wrong about the facts in Example 1, it is not focused enough on the extract or the novel, and concentrates so much on the context that it turns into something of a History essay.

Example 2, on the other hand, integrates an understanding of the novel's context with detailed reference to the extract. In addition, this opening is widening out by the end to deal with the other families included in the initial notes.

Example 2, therefore, is a better English Literature response than Example 1.

### Activity 3

**a.** Look back at the opening you wrote to your essay. Is yours more like Example 1 or Example 2?

**b.** Write down a few sentences about what you have learned from this about writing a source-based response to a 19th-century novel question.

### Support

Plan the rest of your essay, working out what you would include in each paragraph, and write the final paragraph.

**Tip** Try to hold back a good point for your conclusion, so you end on a strong note.

### Stretch

Develop the opening you have just written to a full essay response.

# 6 Looking at the novel as a whole

## Learning objectives

- To gain further practice in close-reading skills
- To focus on the ending of the novel
- To reflect on the novel as a whole

**a.** Look again at the ending of the 19th-century novel you have studied.

**b.** Annotate and make notes on the extract you have chosen, focusing on its style (how it is written).

To help you, look at the example opposite, the ending to *The War of the Worlds* by H. G. Wells. This science-fiction story tells of the south of England being invaded by Martians, in an account told by an anonymous narrator.

Working with a partner, or in a small group, discuss the ending of your novel. Points you may want to consider include:

- How are the characters presented in the ending of the novel? Have they changed? If so, how and why?
- How are the themes of the novel represented in the ending?
- What is the tone of the ending? How do you know?
- Do you find the ending satisfactory? Give reasons why, or why not.
- What about the sort of language used – is it typical of the writer's style in the rest of the novel? Give reasons for what you say.

Before the cylinder fell there was a general persuasion that through all the deep of space no life existed beyond the petty surface of our minute sphere. Now we see further. If the Martians can reach Venus, there is no reason to suppose that the thing is impossible for men, and when the slow cooling of the sun makes this earth uninhabitable, as at last it must do, it may be that the thread of life that has begun here will have streamed out and caught our sister planet within its toils.

*Matter-of-fact tone*

*Acceptance of the inevitability of change*

Dim and wonderful is the vision I have conjured up in my mind of life spreading slowly from this little seed bed of the solar system throughout the inanimate vastness of sidereal[1] space. But that is a remote dream. It may be, on the other hand, that the destruction of the Martians is only a reprieve. To them, and not to us, perhaps, is the future ordained.

*Scientific language*

*Introduction of doubt*

I must confess the stress and danger of the time have left an abiding sense of doubt and insecurity in my mind. I sit in my study writing by lamplight, and suddenly I see again the healing valley below set with writhing flames, and feel the house behind and about me empty and desolate. I go out into the Byfleet Road, and vehicles pass me, a butcher boy in a cart, a cabful of visitors, a workman on a bicycle, children going to school, and suddenly they become vague and unreal, and I hurry again with the artilleryman through the hot, brooding silence. Of a night I see the black powder darkening the silent streets, and the contorted bodies shrouded in that layer; they rise upon me tattered and dog-bitten. They gibber and grow fiercer, paler, uglier, mad distortions of humanity at last, and I wake, cold and wretched, in the darkness of the night.

*Present tense – sense of immediacy*

*Specific place name – suggests normality*

*Disturbing imagery*

*Images of everyday life (children suggest vulnerability)*

*Sudden shift into uncertainty*

*Nightmare imagery*

I go to London and see the busy multitudes in Fleet Street and the Strand, and it comes across my mind that they are but the ghosts of the past, haunting the streets that I have seen silent and wretched, going to and fro, phantasms in a dead city, the mockery of life in a galvanised[2] body. And strange, too, it is to stand on Primrose Hill, as I did but a day before writing this last chapter, to see the great province of houses, dim and blue through the haze of the smoke and mist, vanishing at last into the vague lower sky, [...] to see the sight-seers about the Martian machine that stands there still, to hear the tumult of playing children, and to recall the time when I saw it all bright and clear-cut, hard and silent, under the dawn of that last great day...

*Back to reality?*

*Makes it all seem very real*

*More sense of uncertainty*

*Suggests doubt*

And strangest of all is it to hold my wife's hand again, and to think that I have counted her, and that she has counted me, among the dead.

*Final word 'dead' – significant?*

*Ambivalent ending – happy or not?*

[1]sidereal: star-filled          [2]galvanised: brought into life

---

**Notes**

Everyday, familiar life contrasted with horrific images

General sense of uncertainty

Feeling of doubt, and the threat of being taken over by aliens/outsiders

Scientific terminology

## Exam link

Remember that in the exam, it is important to write about the text and *not* the film!

## Activity 3

You may have seen film versions of the 19th-century novel you have studied.

**a.** If you have, spend some time thinking about to what extent the film version is true to the text. Even with versions quite loyal to the original text, there are likely to be differences (maybe even between different film versions of the same novel).

**b.** Discuss what these differences are, and how they affect the overall impact of the text.

## Activity 4

Write a review of the 19th-century novel you have studied, to be included in a handbook for future GCSE English Literature students.

Points you may want to include:

- what the novel is about: its basic storyline

- the themes of the novel: the ideas the writer may have wanted his or her readers to think about

- the main characters: what they are like, and your thoughts on the ways they speak and behave (you can give your honest opinions of them here!)

- the way it is written: the sort of language used and the way it is structured

- your response to the novel: did you enjoy it? Why, or why not? Any advice you would give to someone coming across it for the first time?

**Progress check**

By now you should be fully confident in your knowledge and understanding of the 19th-century novel you have studied, and how to show this in the exam. Use the questions in the table below as a guide to check that this is the case.

| | Yes ✓ | No ✗ | Maybe ? |
|---|---|---|---|
| I can sum up the main story of the novel in a few sentences. | | | |
| I know the main events in the novel – covering the beginning, the middle, and the end. | | | |
| I know the stories of the main characters – covering the beginning, the middle, and the end. | | | |
| I know about the minor characters, and how they add to the story. | | | |
| I know about the main settings of the story, and how they are important. | | | |
| I know the main themes of the novel, and how they are shown. | | | |
| I understand the context (or contexts) of the novel, and how they are presented. | | | |
| I can refer closely to details from printed extracts and show how they are important. | | | |

# 5 Unseen poetry

In this section of the book, you will develop the skills you need to write about and compare two 'unseen' poems. 'Unseen' means that you are unlikely to have read the poems before, so you have to develop your understanding and make your own responses. This may seem a bit daunting, but once you get used to it, it can be quite liberating. As long as you explain your responses sensibly, and give reasons for your ideas, you can't go wrong.

You will get plenty of practice at these skills. You will start with single poems, until you can independently and confidently analyse them, saying:

● what they are about, i.e. what their content is
● what their themes might be
● how they are written.

Then you will move on to comparing and contrasting pairs of poems.

## Assessment Objectives

In this part of the exam, you will be assessed against these Assessment Objectives:

● **AO1** Read, understand and respond to the texts, maintaining a critical style, developing a personal response, and using textual references, including quotations, to support and illustrate interpretations

● **AO2** Analyse the language, form and structure used by a writer to create meanings and effects, using relevant subject terminology where appropriate

Alongside these Assessment Objectives, you need to compare and contrast the poems.

## In the exam

In two separate questions you will be asked to write about each poem and its effect on you. When you write about the second poem, you will be asked to compare it with the first.

You will be given some guidelines to help you consider:

● the content and structure of the poems – what they are about and how they are organized
● the messages, or themes, the poets may have wanted the reader to think about
● the poets' choices of words, phrases and images and the effects of these
● how you respond to the poems.

You should spend about an hour on this section, and you need to organize this time sensibly. It may help to divide it into roughly:

● 20 minutes on the first poem (including reading and making notes on it)
● 40 minutes on the second poem (including reading and making notes on it, and comparing it with the first poem).

# Working out what a poem is about

## Getting started

In the exam, take note of any bullet points or general guidance in the question.

Take note of the poem's title. It may be really straightforward or it may give you an idea about the messages or themes of the poem. Then read the poem quickly, to get the gist of it.

Now sort out the story, or meaning, of the poem. This is probably the most important stage, so don't rush it! Forget it's a poem for a moment, and divide it into units of sense, rather than reading line by line. Read from punctuation mark to punctuation mark, as if it were a story. This should also help you see if the ideas in the poem develop or change.

Many people make the mistake of treating a poem as a riddle with a deep, hidden meaning. There may well be meanings that are not directly expressed (the 'subtext') and require you to 'read between the lines'. But the only way to understand these is to start at the surface, or most obvious, reading.

Often the most important message comes right at the end of the poem, so pay particular attention to the last few lines. Ask yourself why you think the poet wrote the poem, or what they may have wanted the reader to think about.

You will now have formed an impression of the poem's key messages or themes, so jot these down.

## Getting to detail

Now look at the way the poem is written. This involves looking closely at words, phrases and details, including the way the poem is structured and organized, and always explaining how the bits you have selected add to the overall impact of the messages.

As you're reading in more detail, underline key words or phrases throughout the poem. Aim to make these phrases as brief as possible, as they will end up being your quotations – short quotations are much more effective than long ones.

In the exam, you may be unsure what some words mean – if so, look to see if any help has been given (sometimes indicated by an asterisk). If not, don't worry: you can usually work out the general meaning of a word by looking at its context (what's around it).

Make sure you can say how the words and phrases you selected are effective, and how they help to deliver the message. You should use technical terms where relevant, but just identifying techniques is pointless without showing that you understand how they work. Remember that 'imagery' is a technical term that covers a range of techniques.

## Giving your own ideas and responses

Your personal response is important, so give it! For example, the poem may have reminded you of a personal experience, or something else you have read or seen.

Remember that your ideas are valid, as long as you make a good case, and have followed these guidelines. If you use words like 'perhaps', it shows you're aware that there are different ways of interpreting poems, and are being tentative in your judgements.

# 1 Responding to an unseen poem

## Learning objective

- To develop confidence in reading and interpreting a poem independently

Now it's time to put the theories on pages 118–9 into practice.

### Activity 1

Working either on your own, or with someone else, read and make notes on the poem 'Nothing' by James Fenton.

As you read it, write notes on:

- what the poem is about
- the **themes** or ideas the poet may have wanted you to think about
- the way it is written – this may include the way it is structured or organized, key words or **images**, and so on
- your responses to the poem as a whole.

### Nothing

I take a jewel from a junk-shop tray
And wish I had a love to buy it for.
Nothing I choose will make you turn my way.
Nothing I give will make you love me more.

I know that I've embarrassed you too long
And I'm ashamed to linger at your door.
Whatever I embark on will be wrong.
Nothing I do will make you love me more.

I cannot work. I cannot read or write.
How can I frame a letter to implore.
Eloquence is a lie. The truth is trite.
Nothing I say will make you love me more.

So I replace the jewel in the tray
And laughingly pretend I'm far too poor.
Nothing I give, nothing I do or say,
Nothing I am will make you love me more.

James Fenton

### Support

a. This poem is written in the **first person** ('I') and addressed to another person ('you'). What is the effect of this?

b. Count the number of times the word 'Nothing' is used. Why do you think the poet has repeated this word so often?

c. What do you think the speaker's feelings are in the poem (sometimes called 'the voice', as it may not necessarily be the poet)? How do you know?

d. What do you think is the effect of the reference to the 'jewel' in a 'junk-shop tray'?

## Stretch

a. See how succinctly you can complete this sentence, while still summing up the key essence of the poem: '"Nothing" by James Fenton is about…'

b. The structure of this poem is very contained, with a regular rhyme scheme and pattern of **stanzas**. What might the effects of this be, in your opinion? How might it contribute to the overall impact of the poem?

c. Look closely at how the poem builds up to the final two lines – what do you make of this ending to the poem?

Now, put what you've learned from discussing 'Nothing' into exploring another poem, 'Zero Hour', by Matthew Sweeney.

## Activity 2

Although 'Zero Hour' is a very different type of poem, the same principles apply, so try to read and annotate (make notes on) it. Think about:

a. What is the situation here? What is going on?

b. What are the mood and atmosphere in the poem? How do you know? Do they change at all? If so, where, how, and why?

c. What is the effect of the poem being written in the present tense (as if it's happening as we read it)?

d. What are the effects of the questions in the final stanza?

e. What words and phrases do you find effective? Try to choose two or three in each stanza and explain how they are effective in the poem as a whole.

f. Most of the last stanza is composed of one sentence – how do you think this may contribute to the mood and atmosphere of the poem as a whole?

g. What is your response to the poem?

### Zero Hour

Tomorrow all the trains will stop
and we will be stranded. Cars
have already been immobilized
by the petrol wars, and sit
abandoned, along the roadsides.
The airports, for two days now,
are closed-off zones where dogs
congregate loudly on the runways.

To be in possession of a bicycle
is to risk your life. My neighbour,
a doctor, has somehow acquired a horse
and rides to his practice, a rifle
clearly visible beneath the reins,
I sit in front of the television
for each successive news bulletin
then reach for the whisky bottle.

How long before the shelves are empty
in the supermarkets? The first riots
are raging as I write, and who
out there could have predicted
this sudden countdown to zero hour,
all the paraphernalia of our comfort
stamped obsolete, our memories
fighting to keep us sane and upright?

Matthew Sweeney

# 2 Analysing sample responses

## Learning objectives

- To develop awareness of the features of an effective response to unseen poetry
- To develop the required skills for writing a response to unseen poems

### Activity 1

Now look at these examples of approaches to 'Zero Hour'. Which of these two openings do you think is the more effective, and why?

**Response 1**

In 'Zero Hour', Matthew Sweeney says how all the trains are stopping and cars are abandoned. Even to have a bicycle is risky, so people are just sitting in their houses and drinking whisky while watching the news on television.

**Response 2**

In 'Zero Hour', Matthew Sweeney creates a picture of a familiar world, where everything we take for granted, such as means of transport, seems to be coming to an end, and disorder is spreading.

If you chose Response 2, that's the right answer, as this has more of an **overview** of the whole poem, while Response 1 is just **paraphrasing** so does not show as much understanding.

Now look at different approaches to writing about stylistic features in 'Zero Hour'.

**Response 1**

The poem is written in the first person, and uses dramatic verbs like 'immobilized', 'abandoned', 'closed-off', 'risk', 'raging', 'stamped obsolete.' This makes it very dramatic and frightening for the reader. The poet also uses rhetorical questions like 'How long before the shelves are empty/in the supermarkets?' and 'and who/out there could have predicted/this sudden countdown to zero hour, all the paraphernalia of our comfort/stamped obsolete, our memories/fighting to keep us sane and upright?' These are rhetorical questions because the poet does not expect an answer.

**Response 2**

The poet creates a sense of immediacy, by writing in the first person and the present tense: 'The first riots/are raging as I write.' This puts the reader in the position of the central character and highlights the increasing sense of chaos of the situation described in the poem. The first stanza emphasizes the feeling of everything stopping and people being isolated, with its reference to people being 'stranded' and cars being 'immobilized' and 'abandoned' as a result of the 'petrol wars.' Even familiar places, like airports, are portrayed as frightening, 'closed-off zones' with dogs apparently running wild. This all makes for an extreme sense of insecurity.

Response 1 makes some valid, although rather general points. It shows some awareness of stylistic features (although all the words selected are not, in fact, verbs – 'obsolete', for example) but it doesn't develop them. Selecting and listing quotations will not get you very far if you do not explain how they fit into the story of the poem, and how they work to develop its ideas. Identifying stylistic features, as has been done with rhetorical questions here, is insufficient in itself, if you do not explore their impact on the poem as a whole. In addition, the quotations are much too long. Quote only the word/s that really illustrate your point.

Response 2 starts out with a clear overview, about the sense of immediacy, and this is then supported by appropriate use of technical terms, like 'first person' and 'stanza', with chosen detail of words and phrases being integrated into the discussion, so it makes clear sense.

Notice how, after a close focus on words and their effects, this part of the response pulls back again to end with an overview: 'This all makes for an extreme sense of insecurity'. This technique of overview, followed by close, specific detail, and then widening out again, is a good way of showing your appreciation of how a text is effective.

## Activity ②

Now try writing your own response to 'Zero Hour', putting into practice what you have learned so far. If it helps, you can follow on from the start provided in Response 2.

### Support

Create a poster for 'Zero Hour'. Aim to suggest its mood and atmosphere and themes in your design.

### Stretch

Imagine that 'Zero Hour' is being made into a short film, to help students who are studying it.

Write a proposal for the film company, suggesting how its key ideas, mood and atmosphere and themes could be conveyed to an audience.

Think, for example, about presentation of setting and characters, and appropriate background music.

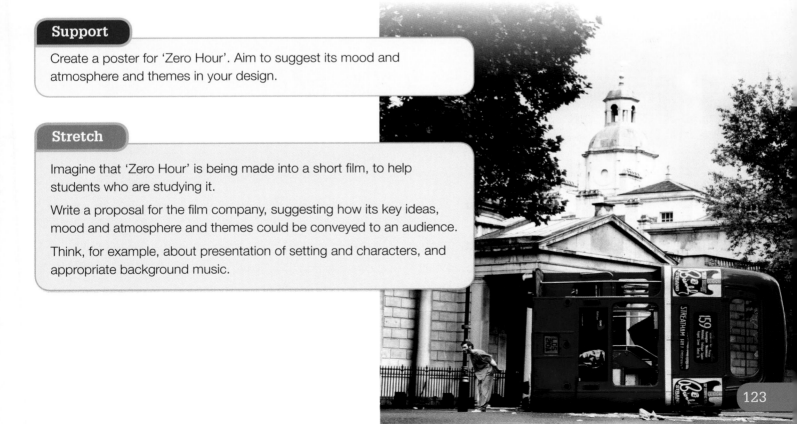

# 3 What makes an effective unseen poetry response?

## Learning objectives

- To develop an understanding of what makes a good response to an unseen poetry question, by exploring a series of examples
- To practise the skills for analysing unseen poems

Now we will look more closely at what makes a good response to an unseen poem.

## Activity 1

Either on your own or in a small group, read the poem 'Shopkeeper', by Greg Hill, and respond to the questions that come after it.

### Shopkeeper

*What a quiet time of year*
he told me, for it was February
and the trees were bare.

Storms had blown even beech leaves
from hedges not a week before
and trees were down at the forest eaves.

What he meant by quiet was a lack
of visitors coming and going on the forest road,
stopping to buy in his shop full of tack.

He said it with his foot just inches
from patches of snowdrops blooming between
daffodil shoots and yards from the bird-table flurry of
tits and finches.

In the distance the mountains glittered with snow.
His van was in neutral, its engine revving
with gathering speed. I watched him go.

I thought yes, how quiet it seems.
The sun glistened a dew-wet web in the hedge
and hushed the cold rush of the roaring streams.

Greg Hill

**a.** Two people are mentioned in this poem – what impressions do you get of each of them?

**b.** What impressions do you get of the place where the poem is set?

**c.** What do you think the poet may have wanted readers to think about?

**d.** Highlight words and phrases that you find effective in putting across the messages or themes of the poem, and explain why you think they are effective.

**Support**

Make a poster of this poem. You may choose to illustrate it with your own drawings, or choose photos or illustrations to create a collage.

**Stretch**

a. Track the changing **tone** in the poem, noting how, and where, it changes.

b. What do you think about the final stanza of the poem? Look closely here at the poet's use of language and its effects.

Now, read the following students' responses to Greg Hill's poem, 'Shopkeeper'.

**Response 1**

The title of the poem 'Shopkeeper' is simple and tells us what the poem is about. The poem is set out in regular verses. Each verse flows from the beginning to the end of it. It is finished by full stops. In each verse the first and third lines rhyme and it is written in the first person which makes it more personal and appealing to the reader.

The poet, Greg Hill, uses italics when writing what the shop keeper was saying, this makes it clearer to differentiate between the people who are talking to the reader.

In the first verse he sets the scene, it is February and how everything has dropped off the trees. But as the poem progresses we see the change in seasons. I think the poet intends us to see that the shopkeeper is talking about people and how quiet it is as there are no visitors (people) but the poet sees that the place was bursting with life. The words the poet uses to describe the nature are not quiet. He uses **onomatopoeia** 'hushed the cold rush of the roaring streams'. This allows us to hear the sounds of the natural elements of this poem. He also uses **alliteration** when writing 'dew-wet web'.

I like this poem as it is clever. I think that the description the poet uses brings it to life and creates a picture in my mind of how I would imagine this place.

**Response 2**

The poem is about the absurdity of the first line: 'What a quiet time of year.' The author has heard this statement from a shopkeeper, and he comments on how this man must be deaf. Words such as 'revving', 'roaring' and 'flurry', imply noise and movement. He seems to be saying that to the naked eye, 'the trees were bare', and it was quiet, but if the shopkeeper had looked in detail at things he had seen so many times before, it was a truly bustling time of year. 'He said it with his foot just inches from patches of snowdrops.' Greg Hill seems to be incredulous that someone can see the 'flurry of tits and finches' and hear 'the cold rush of the roaring streams', and still make such a statement.

He may have wanted us to consider the meaning of the word 'quiet'. He understands that what the shopkeeper 'meant by quiet was a lack of visitors' at his shop. He feels, however, that the shopkeeper has misinterpreted the meaning of the word 'quiet'. While trade may be a little slow, there are so many things happening at this time of year that the shopkeeper is deaf and blind to: 'In the distance the mountains glittered with snow.' He seems to be saying that there are so many beautiful, wonderful things happening at this time of year, but people like the shopkeeper just don't appreciate them anymore.

The poem seems to be full of wonder at the magnificence of nature: 'glistened', 'glittered'. Everything seems breathtaking, yet unsubstantial. He also creates a mood of sarcasm. 'I thought yes, how quiet it seems.' This seems to have been written jokingly, almost mockingly, for while the shopkeeper feels it's quiet at this time of year, Greg Hill can see and hear so much more.

The title, 'Shopkeeper', is something artificial, removed from nature. This seems to hint that humans have become removed from nature, and can no longer revel in it. Each stanza has three long lines, as though Greg Hill is trying to pack in as much of his emotion at the beauty of nature as he can. Stanzas three and four seem to contrast, stanza three talking about the worthless 'tack' that his shop is full of, while stanza four is full of beautiful imagery, 'patches of snowdrops blooming', 'daffodil shoots', 'bird-table flurry'. It is as though all of human technology will never compare to the grace of nature, and when put in comparison, the shopkeeper's store seems worthless. The short sentence, 'I watched him go' seems to highlight Greg Hill's views completely. He watches, he observes, he drinks in the wonder of the world about him.

Also, the shopkeeper takes the trees being bare as evidence for it being a quiet time of year. Unlike Greg Hill, he never took the time to observe that the trees were bare because 'storms had blown even beech leaves from hedges.' He is saying that everything in nature has a cause, if only people could be bothered to look for it.

Finally, the poem had quite an effect on me. It made me realize that people don't enjoy nature any more, we take everything for granted. It alerted me to the beauty that could be found every day, as long as I stopped ignoring what was right in front of me, and took an interest in my surroundings instead.

## Activity 2

Working on your own or with a partner, write a list of what makes Response 2 a stronger response than Response 1. Obviously, Response 2 is much longer, but there's more to it than that! Think about:

- the opening of each response – how do they differ?
- the focus on stylistic features (language, form and structure) and their effects
- how the writer of each response makes clear their understanding of the poem
- how the writers show their personal response to the possible messages of the poem
- the way each writer uses quotations.

### A summary of some of the points you may have considered

The writer of Response 1 shows some awareness of what the poem is about, but does so in general terms and tends to 'spot' or just identify stylistic features, as in, 'He also uses alliteration when writing "dew-wet web".' This is opposed to tracking through the poem, selecting and highlighting key words and phrases in order to discuss how they are effective in putting across the poet's ideas.

By contrast, the writer of Response 2 is clearly focused throughout on the effect of the way the poem is written, and, therefore, how the poet has conveyed his ideas. Short quotations have been carefully chosen and are always linked to a clear point. Notice also how the writer has integrated quotations into their own sentences.

# A high-achieving response

Finally, read this very assured response to the same poem, alongside the comments that highlight its strengths.

Hits the ground running, with a clear overview ············▶

The poem 'Shopkeeper' by Greg Hill is a poignant comment on the common human inability to appreciate the beauty of the world around them, and the tendency to see the problems in a situation and ignore the wonders that surround us. Hill talks of how a shopkeeper has failed to notice the 'snowdrops blooming' or the way the 'sun glistened', and is instead concerned by the 'lack of visitors' stopping at his shop – a materialistic contrast to the purity of the natural world.

Sums up main content and ideas of the poem ············▶

I think Hill wanted us to consider the way in which we let the world pass us by, and fail to appreciate the extraordinary beauty and wonderful sounds of our surroundings. It could be suggested that Hill is calling for the reader to slow down, to stop the metaphorical 'engine revving' of our daily lives and consider our good fortune to simply be alive and be blessed with the world we inhabit.

Informed personal response ············▶

Well integrated reference to stylistic features ············▶

This poem has a pensive mood, designed to provoke thought and inspire reflection in the reader. To create this contemplative atmosphere the poet has slowed the pace of reading with the use of elongated vowel sounds, such as those in 'beech leaves' and later in 'blooming', and prevents the reader from beginning the poem too quickly with a **caesura** in the second line: 'he told me, for it was February'. I find that the poem's mood also carries a touch of melancholy, perhaps created by the recurrent references to the trees being 'bare' and the repetition of the 'quiet' atmosphere in the forest.

## Key terms

**Caesura:** deliberate short break or pause within a line

**Assonance:** repetition of vowel sounds for effect

**Enjambement:** where the sense runs from one line to the next without a pause

The images described in the poem are beautifully created through a number of techniques. Hill has carefully selected words such as 'flurry' to recreate the busy yet light movements of the tiny birds around the bird-table and the word 'glittered' perfectly captures the sparkling light of the February sun upon the snow. Hill's onomatopoeic use of the words 'hushed' and 'rushed' emphasize the gentle sounds of the streams in the forest, and, indeed, the **assonance** of these two words further allow the reader to imagine the sounds of the 'roaring streams.' I also find the contrast between the mundane, everyday vocabulary used in the second stanza to describe the shopkeeper's attitude to be interestingly contrasted with the poet's carefully selected imagery to describe the sights and sounds in the forest.

More appreciation of style and effect, with accurate use of terminology, and really close discussion of words

Structurally, I feel that Hill is commenting on how such extraordinary and beautiful things can be viewed as so commonplace and normal, and it could be suggested that it is for this reason that Hill has chosen to house such perfect imagery and description in such a plain, regimented form of regular stanzas. It is also possible that the **enjambement** used is designed to echo the seamless transition of the natural world through the seasons.

Confident discussion of structure and form

I like this poem because it has posed some interesting philosophical questions on the way we view the world and whether we should be so materialistic, or simply enjoy our surroundings.

Strong personal response to conclude

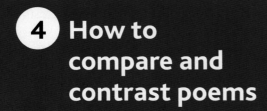

# 4 How to compare and contrast poems

## Learning objective

- To develop the skills for comparing and contrasting two poems

Now it's time to move on to the next stage, showing how poems are similar and how they are different.

Working either on your own or with someone else, read and make notes on the following pair of poems, 'On Ageing' by Maya Angelou and 'Another Small Incident' by David Sutton. Both poems describe attitudes to old age. Use the 'points to consider' following the poems to help you make your notes.

### On Ageing

When you see me sitting quietly,
Like a sack left on the shelf,
Don't think I need your chattering,
I'm listening to myself.
Hold! Stop! Don't pity me!
Hold! Stop your sympathy!
Understanding if you got it,
Otherwise I'll do it without it!

When my bones are stiff and aching
And my feet won't climb the stairs,
I will only ask one favour:
Don't bring me no rocking chair.

When you see me walking, stumbling,
Don't study and get it wrong.
'Cause tired don't mean lazy
And every goodbye ain't gone.
I'm the same person I was back then,
A little less hair, a little less chin,
A lot less lungs and much less wind,
But ain't I lucky I can still breathe in.

Maya Angelou

### Points to consider

- Deal with each poem separately at first – sort out the story, or meaning, of each one.
- Think about the point of view presented in each poem.
- What do you think is the attitude of the people featured in each poem? How do you know?
- Look at the way the poems are structured or organized – how does this help to convey the messages of the poems?
- Focus closely on the words, phrases and images used in each poem and think about how they are effective.
- Think about which of the two poems has the most impact on you, and why. Is it because of the content, the message, the way it is written, the use of stylistic features, or a mix of all these things?

### Another Small Incident

November evening, rain outside and dark
Beyond the building's honeycomb of warmth.
The old man stands there, waiting to be noticed.
He wears propitiation[1] like a coat.
The girl looks up at him. 'Yes? Can I help you?'
'This card you sent like, that's the problem, see.
It says I've got your book, but that's not right.
I mean, I had it but I brought it back.
That's what I do, I read one, bring it back.
I never keep them, see.'
                              He stands, condemned
Yet quivering for justice. 'All right sir.'
She smiles at him. 'We get mistakes like that.
Just leave the card with me.' He stares at her,
Seventy, with spotted hands, afraid,
And someone smiles at him and calls him sir.
Lighting at the contact, like a bulb,
He warms to her. 'That's what I do, you see.
I take the one, I read it, bring it back.
I thought, you know, it might be on the shelves.
I mean, if no one's had it since like, see.'
Another girl comes by. 'We're closing, Sue.
You coming?' Sue looks up and rolls her eyes.
The old man catches it. He understands.
He turns and shuffles out into the night.

David Sutton

[1] propitiation: needing to be forgiven

> **Tip** Remember that reading from punctuation mark to punctuation mark helps you to sort out the story of a poem.

- 'On Ageing' is written in a direct way, as if the speaker is addressing the reader. How is this effective?
- There are quite a lot of negative references in both poems – think about how they are used in each poem.
- How significant is the use of dialect in the Angelou poem?
- How effective is the use of direct speech in the Sutton poem?
- Focus on the use of contrast in both poems, and how it is used.
- Think about the use of imagery in each poem, and how it conveys the possible themes of both poems.
- Look closely at how the ideas are developed in each poem, paying particular attention to how they end.

## Your turn at comparing and contrasting

Now it's your turn to have a go at comparing and contrasting the two poems about attitudes to old age, 'On Ageing' by Maya Angelou and 'Another Small Incident' by David Sutton.

### Activity 2

First, write about 'On Ageing' by Maya Angelou, and its effect on you.

You might consider:

- what the poem is about and how it is organized
- the ideas the poet may have wanted us to think about
- the poet's choice of words, phrases and images and the effects they create
- how you respond to the poem.

Next, write about 'Another Small Incident', by David Sutton, and show how it is similar to and different from 'On Ageing'. Consider the same points as you considered for 'On Ageing' and also the similarities and differences between 'On Ageing' and 'Another Small Incident'.

### Support

What are the three main points of advice you would give to someone about to start comparing and contrasting unseen poems? Use your own experience to decide what advice you think is important and helpful.

### Stretch

Find a pair of poems that are linked in some way by theme, and make notes on what you could say about each poem, and the points of similarity and difference between them.

**Tip**

When writing about similarities and differences, you need to use words like 'similarly' and 'also' for similarities and 'whereas' and 'on the other hand' for differences. How many other words and phrases can you think of for comparing and contrasting? Make a list of them, and aim to use a range in your response.

### Exam link

In the exam there are 15 marks for writing about the first poem, and 25 marks for writing about the second, and comparing it with the first, so you need to make sure that you use your time wisely. Aim to spend about 20 minutes on the first poem, and about 40 minutes on the second one (including comparing it with the first).

## Progress check

Once you have finished your response on the 'ageing' poems, use the following checklist to see how well you have done. If you can say 'yes' to most of these points, you're definitely on the right track!

| | Yes ✓ | No ✗ |
| --- | --- | --- |
| Have you started strongly, maybe with an overview of both poems? | | |
| Have you written in detail about both poems? | | |
| Have you avoided paraphrasing and making general points? | | |
| Are the points you have made clearly supported with evidence from the poems? | | |
| Have you looked closely at *how* the poets put their messages across, using language, form and structure? | | |
| Have you used technical terminology relevantly, and in context? Remember, just spotting features won't get you far at all. | | |
| Are your quotations brief, while still making sense within your sentences? | | |
| Does the detail you've selected fit into the overview? | | |
| Have you written in detail about sensible similarities and differences between both poems, addressing their content, messages and how they are written? | | |
| Have you given a confident personal response to both poems? | | |

# 5 What makes an effective unseen poetry comparison?

## Learning objective

- To learn to discriminate between different levels of response in a poetry comparison task

 **Tip** Remember the stages of reading and annotating:

1. Read each poem once to get the gist, and to take note of any help given in the question – this may be pretty quick.

2. Read each poem again more thoroughly, to sort out the story, by reading in units of sense.

3. Read each poem a third time to select and highlight detail, looking closely at how the poem is written.

4. Jot down the key points you want to compare.

## Activity 1

Now you have had a go at comparing and contrasting two unseen poems, you should be in a better position to identify what makes a successful response.

You are going to read three responses to two poems about individuals who appear to be rejected by society: 'Tramp', by Rupert M. Loydell, and 'Decomposition', by Zulfikar Ghose.

First of all, read the question and the poems below, making notes.

> (a) **Write about 'Tramp' by Rupert M. Loydell, and its effect on you. You may wish to consider:**
> - what the poem is about and how it is organized
> - the ideas the poet may have wanted us to think about
> - the poet's choice of words, phrases and images and the effects they create
> - how you respond to the poem.
>
> (b) **Now compare 'Tramp' by Rupert M. Loydell and 'Decomposition' by Zulfikar Ghose. You should compare:**
> - what the poems are about and how they are organized
> - the ideas the poets may have wanted us to think about
> - the poets' choice of words, phrases and images and the effects they create
> - how you respond to the poems.

### Tramp

This mad prophet
gibbers mid-traffic,
wringing his hands
whilst mouthing at heaven.

No messages for us.
His conversation is simply
a passage through time.
he points and calls.

Our uneven stares dissuade[1]
approach. We fear him, his
matted hair, patched coat,
grey look from sleeping out.

We mutter amongst ourselves
and hope he keeps away. No
place for him in our heaven,
there it's clean and empty.

Rupert M. Loydell

[1] dissuade: persuade against

## Decomposition

I have a picture I took in Bombay
of a beggar asleep on the pavement:
grey-haired, wearing shorts and a dirty shirt,
his shadow thrown aside like a blanket.

His arms and legs could be cracks in the stone;
routes for the ants' journeys, the flies' descents.
brain-washed by the sun into exhaustion,
he lies veined into stone, a fossil man.

Behind him, there is a crowd passingly
bemused by a pavement trickster and quite
indifferent to this very common sight
of an old man asleep on the pavement.

I thought it was a good composition
and glibly called it The Man in the Street,
remarking how typical it was of
India that the man in the street lived there.

His head in the posture of one weeping
into a pillow chides me[1] now for my
presumption at attempting to compose
art out of his hunger and solitude.

Zulfikar Ghose

[1] chides me: tells me off

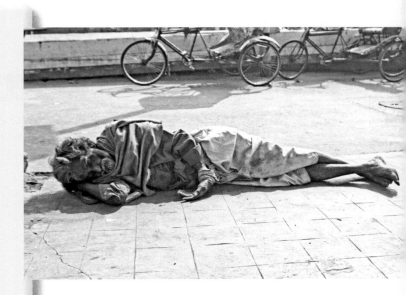

**Key term**

**Simile:** a comparison or similarity between two things that are otherwise not similar; it always contains the word 'like' or 'as'

# Identifying a strong response

Below are three responses to the exam question on 'Tramp' and 'Decomposition' on page 134.

## Activity 2

Read the students' responses, along with the annotations. When you have done this, put the three responses into a rank order, with a brief explanation of the strengths and possible areas for improvement for each.

**Response 1**

(a) In the poem, 'Tramp', the poet describes a tramp on the streets and how people react to him. He describes the homeless person as something to fear, 'Our uneven stares dissuade approach. We fear him.' This shows the reader that they try to avoid the man because of fear. The poem describes the reaction to individuals on the edge of society to be negative, people are not friendly towards them. 'We mutter amongst ourselves and hope he keeps away.' This shows that people are prejudiced towards the homeless and are judgemental towards them, not knowing the reasons why they are there.

The poet of 'Tramp' may have wanted us to think about how people feel about the life of a homeless man. 'This mad prophet gibbers mid-traffic' shows that he is in the way and that he talks nonsense, that there is no point of him speaking. The label of being 'homeless' is a bad thing that people look down on you for.

I think 'Tramp' is quite pessimistic. It shows the hatred of the homeless and shows the negative impact it might have on others. 'No place for him in our heaven, there it's clean and empty.' This in the last stanza is thought-provoking, making you think why people are so judgemental towards others.

*Clear focus*

*Some discussion and awareness*

*Personal response*

*Strong personal response to message*

## Points to consider

Ask yourself these questions when you are considering each response:

- How well has the student understood 'the story' of each poem and how it is structured or organized?

- Has the student understood the possible messages of each poem – the ideas the poets may have wanted us to think about?

- Is there a thoughtful discussion of each poem?

- Do the selections and highlighting of details from both poems focus on *how* the messages are put across?

- Is there a sensible, confident, and accurate use of technical terms?

- Is the response well structured with a clear introduction, conclusion, and links between the poems?

- Is there a developed discussion of similarities and differences between the poems?

(b) In the poem 'Decomposition' the poet describes people's reactions to a tramp as being quite varied, 'quite indifferent to this common sight.' This poem shows that people who live on the street are usually common, the **simile** 'his shadow, thrown aside like a blanket' shows the reader that this man is not valued, being 'thrown aside', like a piece of rubbish. Also, the poet may have wanted us to think about the 'art out of his hunger and solitude', he is trying to make us think about the art of homelessness.

*Quotation doesn't quite fit the point made*

*Some discussion of imagery and effect*

The beggar in 'Decomposition' wears 'a dirty shirt.' This shows that he is not well presented, being dirty, this isn't pleasant. This poem is also thought-provoking. 'He lies veined into stone, a fossil man.' This quotation makes the atmosphere of the poem interesting, using imagery.

*Simple judgement*

*General comment – doesn't discuss meaning or effects*

Both the poems 'Tramp' and 'Decomposition' are about describing people's reactions to individuals on the edge of society. Both poems want us to think about the lives of tramps and beggars. Both poems describe the homeless men to be unliked, but I think that Zulfikar Ghose was trying to explain the art of homelessness whereas Rupert M. Loydell was trying to get the reader to think about how people despise the homeless.

*Comparison begins*

*Attempt to compare, in rather general terms*

Both poems are quite pessimistic. They both show how passers-by react to the homeless. In both poems they tend to ignore the homeless men. Both poems use effective words and phrases. In 'Tramp' the phrase I found most interesting was 'chides me.' I found this interesting because the word 'chides' makes you think and puts you in deep thought about the words you read. In 'Decomposition' the phrase I found most interesting was 'a fossil man' because fossils are a type of stone.

*Only simple comments on language*

Both poems are written in a negative way, and both are about males. In 'Tramp' 'his matted hair' shows it is about a male. In 'Decomposition', 'The Man in the Street' shows it is about a male.

*Very simple comparison*

In my opinion, my favourite poem is 'Decomposition', mainly because it is more thought-provoking and it gives you an insight into homelessness in Bombay. Both poems have differences and similarities but 'Tramp' I found was written in a more pessimistic way. The reactions to individuals on the edge of society can be seen in different ways. Zulfikar Ghose thought of it more as art whereas Rupert M. Loydell thought that homeless people were despised. Neither poems explored the reasons of homelessness and both were judgemental.

*Personal response to both poems*

*Sensible points about similarities and differences*

**Response 2**

(a) The poem 'Tramp' illustrates the poignant life of a homeless man who spends a substantial amount of time doing nothing of any significance. The slightly derogatory title 'Tramp' suggests that people perceive him as a lower value of man who has achieved little. It is from the point of view of the people who view him on a regular basis and try to avoid him but cannot help but make a social comment, 'No place for him in our heaven.' There is no evidence to suggest that the man has committed any notable crimes to cast a negative light on his seemingly unwanted presence. It denotes that they perceive the 'tramp' as a threat to their 'heaven', 'hope he keeps away.' His actions are interpreted as malicious and possibly having a detrimental effect, 'gibbers,' 'mouthing at heaven.'

The attitudes in this poem could be described as quite passive as there is little sinister language, 'This mad prophet.' The **syntax** of the poem is the same and creates a neutral effect which controls the tone of the poem. There is no obvious rhythm or rhyme to the poem which adds to the detached mood, 'No messages for us.' This man is strange and does not follow the pattern of everyday life, 'mid-traffic', the **colloquial language** used conveys the relaxed and modern atmosphere that the poem creates.

The use of enjambement in the poem, 'His conversation is simply a passage through time' illustrates the passing of time and how it has little effect on the 'tramp.' He seems unaffected and continues to carry out his usual tedious tasks. The visual imagery used, 'matted hair, patched coat, grey look from sleeping out' paints the ideal picture of a typical tramp, there is no abstract imagery to create any unexpected tension. The formulaic structure adds to the monotonous image created by the visual imagery.

I believe that the people have strong religious views on the functioning of society, 'it's clean and empty.' They perceive any outcasts as people who have a negative effect on society and must therefore be avoided, 'We fear him.' The instilling of fear emphasizes this.

Clear overview

Language and effects

Developed and perceptive evaluation

Some valid discussion of style

Confident exploration of style, structure and effects

Personal response, with support

### Key terms

**Syntax:** the way words and phrases are ordered

**Colloquial language:** informal language such as that used in everyday conversation

(b) The poem, 'Decomposition' once again conveys a homeless person but from the perspective of a still image. The photo portrays a 'beggar asleep on the pavement.' Crowds of people are deterred by him like the first poem. The mood of the poem is pensive as the photographer is looking back on the image in a contemplative manner. It evokes pathos through imagery of hunger and solitude, 'arms and legs could be cracks in the stones.' It's slightly metaphorical as it conveys his emaciated body as mere cracks in the stone, the deeper meaning could suggest the little impact that he has on society.

*Clear focus, with link to 'Tramp'*

*Similarity noted*

*Close analysis of style; sensitive appreciation of effects*

The imagery of stone and lack of movement, 'a fossil man' suggests that the photo captured the man doing nothing which is part of his pattern. The title 'Decomposition' denotes that this man is decomposing like a mere plant, he's attributed no emotion and conveyed as an inanimate object. The final stanza shows a change in the tone of the poem, although the rhythm remains the same, he becomes suddenly upset that he did nothing but observe the man 'to compose art out of his hunger and solitude.' It evokes pathos as we can empathize with the man who can do little but watch others suffer.

*Confident and sensitive evaluation of style and effects*

There are many similarities between the two poems, the predominant one is that they are both a portrayal of two homeless people who are shown little compassion, 'Our uneven stares dissuade approach.' People avoid them out of pre-conceived conceptions rather than anything else, 'a crowd passingly bemused by a pavement trickster.' It's evident that people overlook the helpless people in society, this is illustrated continuously through both poems. The difference between the two poems is the extent to which they have suffered, 'grey look from sleeping out.' The visual imagery in the first poem illustrates that the man is only feeling the minor effects. In the second poem the man has suffered much more, 'he lies veined into a stone.' This visual imagery of the scene being vascular emphasized the extent to which the man has been affected, he's embedded in the pavement, 'brainwashed' through no fault of his own. Another similarity is the change that occurs in the final stanza, 'No place for him in our heaven.' The religious allusion conveys how the man is assumed to be an unfit outcast, the second poem's final stanza conveys how the man changes his views. He comments on the social injustice that had caused this 'beggar' to be affected so badly, 'His head in the posture of one weeping.' Only after much contemplation of the image can the man understand how he is powerless to help the 'beggar'. He can only spectate and debate his decision to take the photo.

*Confident, supported comparison*

*Clear highlighting of differences*

*Assured overview of structure and style*

*Well-supported personal response*

## Response 3

(a) In the poem 'Tramp' the poet talks about the devil and describes him as a bad thing 'mad prophet gibbers mid traffic, wringing his hands whilst mouthing at heaven.' This quote shows the devil is described as a bad thing. The **personification** used in 'mad prophet' makes him look bad because he is being described as mad. The alliteration used in 'mad… mid' shows the poet's anger about the devil. The **juxtaposition** used in 'mad prophet' shows that the devil is mad but some people praise him as a prophet which is wrong.

The poet tries to warn people about the devil, 'We fear him, his matted hair, patched coat, grey looking from sleeping out.' This quote shows that we should be scared of the devil as very dark and negative. The alliteration used in 'his hand' shows her worry about the devil.

Probable misreading

Empty, and inaccurate feature-spotting

Simple feature spotting

Confused response

Continued misreading

Confused, empty feature-spotting

### Key terms

**Personification:** making something not alive sound as if it is alive (verb: personify)

**Juxtaposition:** placing two different thing together for contrast

(b) In the poem 'Decomposition' the poet talks about poor people in India and the unfairness in this world, 'grey haired, wearing shorts and dirty shirt, his shadow thrown aside like a blanket. The alliteration of 'sh' shows the poet's anger about how unfair this world is.

*Simple focus*

*Unconvincing comment on style*

The poet tries to make us think about how so many poor people live in this world, called it 'The Man in the Street', remarking how typical it was of India that the man in the street lived there. The repetition of the word 'man' shows that the poet is trying to make us think about that man constantly. The word 'The Man' is written in capital letters at the start of the word to give him respect and honour for living in such conditions.

*Again, unconvincing comment on style*

One difference between the poems is that the atmosphere in the poem 'Tramp' is very scary, 'We mutter amongst ourselves and hope he keeps away.' The alliteration in 'hope he' shows the fear in the atmosphere. The word 'we' makes it personal for us and makes us feel included in the poet's view about the devil.

*valid point, but still based on misreading*

On the other hand, the atmosphere in the poem, 'Decomposition' is very sad and depressed. 'His arms and legs could be cracks in the stone... brain-washed by the sun into exhaustion.' This quote shows that the atmosphere of the poem is very depressed. The alliteration in 'could... crack' shows the sadness and depressed atmosphere.

*Response and awareness*

In my opinion the poet in 'Tramp' shows the typical thinking of the devil a person has, 'no place for him in our heaven, there it's clean and empty.' This quote shows how some people think about the devil. The alliteration in 'him... heaven' shows our anger about the devil.

*Simple personal response based on misreading*

In my opinion the poem 'Decomposition' tries to make us think how lucky we are, 'now for my presumption at attempting to compose art out of his hunger and solitude.' This quote shows how the poet says to fight against hunger in this world. The soft alliteration in 'his hunger' shows us his sadness that he is feeling. The alliteration in 'out of' shows also the worry he has for people that are in hunger.

*Personal interpretation*

*Inaccurate – not alliteration*

If you decided on the following rank order, with 1 being the most effective and 3 the least effective:

Response 1 = 2      Response 2 = 1      Response 3 = 3

you have the right answer!

**Support**

Write a list of handy hints you would give to someone asking for advice on how to go about comparing poems.

**Stretch**

Make notes on what makes Response 2 the one that would get the highest marks.

# 6 Putting it all together

## Learning objective

- To practise skills developed through this section, in an exam-type question

Now it's your chance to see how much you have learned in this section, by independently writing your own response to the following pair of poems, 'The River's Story' by Brian Patten and 'Song of the City' by Gareth Owen.

Read the two poems. They are both about humans' impact on the environment.

### The River's Story

I remember when life was good.
I shilly-shallied across meadows,
Tumbled down mountains,
I laughed and gurgled through woods,
Stretched and yawned in a myriad of floods.
Insects, weightless as sunbeams,
Settled on my skin to drink.
I wore lily-pads like medals.
Fish, lazy and battle-scarred,
Gossiped beneath them.
The damselflies were my ballerinas,
The pike my ambassadors.
Kingfishers, disguised as rainbows,
Were my secret agents.
It was a sweet time, a gone-time,
A time before factories grew,
Brick by greedy brick,
And left me cowering

In monstrous shadows.
Like drunken giants
They vomited their poisons into me.
Tonight a scattering of vagrant bluebells,
Dwarfed by those same poisons,
Toll my ending.
Children, come find me if you wish,
I am your inheritance.
Behind derelict housing-estates
You will discover my remnants.
Clogged with garbage and junk
To an open sewer I've shrunk.

I, who have flowed through history,
Have seen hamlets become villages,
Villages become towns, towns become cities,
Am reduced to a trickle of filth
Beneath the still, burning stars.

Brian Patten

### Song of the City

My brain is stiff with concrete
My limbs are rods of steel
My belly's stuffed with money
My soul was bought in a deal.

They poured metal through my arteries
They choked my lungs with lead
They churned my blood to plastic
They put murder in my head.

I'd a face like the map of the weather
Flesh that grew to the bone
But they tore my story out of my eyes
And turned my heart to stone.

Let me wind from my source like a river
Let me grow like wheat from the grain
Let me hold my arms like a natural tree
Let my children love me again.

Gareth Owen

## Activity ①

**(a) Write about the poem 'The River's Story' by Brian Patten, and its effect on you. You may wish to consider:**

- what the poem is about and how it is organized
- the ideas the poet may have wanted us to think about
- the poet's choice of words, phrases and images and the effects they create
- how you respond to the poem.

## Activity ②

**(b) Now compare 'Song of the City' by Gareth Owen and 'The River's Story' by Brian Patten. You should compare:**

- what the poems are about and how they are organized
- the ideas the poets may have wanted us to think about
- the poets' choice of words, phrases and images and the effects they create
- how you respond to the poems.

## Progress check

By now you should be fully confident in comparing and contrasting two poems you probably will not have read or studied before the exam.
Use the questions below as a guide to check that this is the case.

For each question, answer with:

✓ yes (fully confident)

✗ no (not at all confident – quite a lot of work to be done)

? maybe (a bit more work to be done)

| | Yes ✓ | No ✗ | Maybe ? |
|---|---|---|---|
| I can work out the story of poems, by reading carefully. | | | |
| I can identify the messages of poems; what ideas the poets may have wanted us to think about. | | | |
| I can highlight key words and images and explain how they are effective. | | | |
| I can use technical terms accurately and relevantly. | | | |
| I can express my personal responses to the poems I have read. | | | |
| I can show how poems are similar and different. | | | |
| I can use suitable words to signal that I am comparing or contrasting. | | | |

# GLOSSARY

**Alliteration:** repetition of initial consonants for a specific effect

**Assonance:** repetition of vowel sounds for effect

**Blank verse:** another term for iambic pentameter, with a regular rhythm pattern of ten syllables per line, with the rhythm 'te-dum' for each one (or the stress falling on the second syllable). It is the natural rhythm of spoken English, so often helps to create a conversational tone

**Caesura:** deliberate short break or pause within a line

**Chronologically:** arranged in the order in which events actually happened

**Colloquial:** in an informal style, with language that is used in everyday conversation

**Contemporary:** living or happening at the same time as something else; up to date

**Direct address:** where the poet speaks directly to the reader, using the second person ('you')

**Enjambement:** where the sense of a line carries on from one line to the next, without a pause

**Empathy:** really understanding a character, 'getting under their skin' and feeling for them

**Euphemism:** a way of saying something unpleasant in a nicer, often gentler, way

**First person:** the speaker's point of view, shown by words like 'I', 'me', 'we', 'us'

**Half-rhyme:** exactly what it sounds like: nearly a rhyme, but not quite, like 'keel' and 'beautiful'

**Iambic pentameter:** ten syllables or 'beats' to each line, with the pattern 'te-dum'; it is the rhythm pattern closest to the rhythm of spoken English, so poets often use it to create a conversational tone. It sounds like a steady heartbeat (te-dum; te-dum; te-dum; te-dum; te-dum)

**Iambic tetrameter:** eight-syllable line, with the rhythm 'te-dum'

**Image / imagery:** vivid language (which may include similes, metaphors or personification) to create pictures in words

**Juxtaposition:** placing two different things together for contrast

**Metaphor:** a simile without the words 'like' or 'as' (adjective: metaphorical)

**Monosyllabic:** using single-syllable words

**Octave / octet:** eight lines of poetry, often the first part of a sonnet

**Ode:** a form of poetry with its roots in ancient Greece and Rome. In an ode, the poet addresses an object, or something that cannot answer back

**Onomatopoeia:** 'sound-effect' words – where the word sounds like what it describes

**Overview:** summing up the main ideas, the 'big picture'

**Pace:** the speed at which the text or part of a text is read – it may be quick, slow, or steady, for example

**Paraphrasing:** similar to translating; putting something in your own words without much comment

**Pathetic fallacy:** where the weather, or nature, suggests the mood or feelings of characters

**Personification:** making something not alive sound as if it is alive (verb: personify)

**Petrarchan sonnet:** a sonnet that is divided into two parts, of eight and six lines; it is named after the Italian poet Petrarch

**Proper nouns:** real names of people, places or things

**Romantic movement:** the Romantic poets were writing in the late 18th and early 19th centuries. Their main concern was to make poetry accessible to as many people as possible. Some other qualities were their love of nature and dislike of urban life, an interest in the supernatural and mystical, and in ordinary people

**Second person:** the person the speaker is addressing, shown by the word 'you'

**Sestet:** six lines of poetry, often the second part of a sonnet

**Sibilance:** a sort of hissing sound, created by repeating 's' or 'sh' sounds

**Simile:** where one thing is compared to another using the words 'like' or 'as'

**Soliloquy:** a speech where a character confides their thoughts to the audience, unheard by other characters

**Sonnet:** a traditional poetic form with 14 lines, often split into two parts. It traditionally uses the rhythm of iambic pentameter

**Stage directions:** instructions written into the script of the play, to help actors and people involved in producing the play understand how they should perform the scene in order to convey the characters, mood and atmosphere to an audience

**Stanza:** another word for a verse in poetry

**Succinct:** expressed as briefly as possible

**Synecdoche:** where a part represents the whole (such as 'the hand' for 'the sculptor')

**Syntax:** the way words and phrases are ordered

**Theme:** the text's 'message'; what the writer wants you to think about

**Tone:** the feeling behind what is written. It could be calm, angry, shocked or surprised, for example

**Universal quality:** something that can apply to anyone, at any time or place